The Trial of
Cecil John Rhodes

D1557529

First published by Jacana Media (Pty) Ltd in 2020
Second and third impression 2021

10 Orange Street
Sunnyside
Auckland Park 2092
South Africa
+2711 628 3200
www.jacana.co.za

ISBN 978-1-4314-3079-6

Cover design by Trevor Paul
Editing by Ken Barris
Proofreading by Russell Martin
Set in PSFournier Stf 11/16.45pt
Printed by ABC Press, Cape Town
Job no. 003792

See a complete list of Jacana titles at www.jacana.co.za

The Trial of
Cecil John Rhodes

Adekeye Adebajo

For my sister and spiritual guide

Adefemi Mofolorunso Adebajo (1969–2016)

In Memoriam

Until we meet again in After Africa.

Acknowledgements

My own personal association with the legacy of Cecil Rhodes began in 1990 on winning the single Rhodes Scholarship from Nigeria to study at Oxford University in England. An alarmed uncle – a radical historian – exclaimed at the time: "That thing is dripping with blood. Cecil Rhodes was a brutal imperialist!" My thoughts at the time were more practical: to get a good education at a world-class institution, and if the money of a robber-baron who had plundered Africa's wealth was paying for it, then at least a slice of the treasure was returning to the continent. I felt that I should accept even the crumbs from the great imperialist's gluttonous feast, but promised myself that having completed my studies, I would bite the hand that fed me by pursuing anti-imperial causes and eventually "trying" the self-styled "Colossus": Cecil John Rhodes. This political novella is thus the fulfilment of that promise I made to myself 30 years ago.

I remember my stomach churning at dinners at Rhodes House in Oxford when the assembled dignitaries would turn to a large portrait of the imperialist and raise their glasses to "The Founder." My own silent protest involved refusing to partake in this strange ritual of the most secret of societies. Having obtained the doctoral Golden Fleece from the city of "dreaming spires" and "lost causes" in 1999, I have had two decades to contribute in a small way to anti-colonial initiatives. I have sought to promote Pan-African knowledge-production, the quest for Pax Africana, and a more integrated continent: pursuits that that were the very antithesis of Cecil Rhodes's vision of an imperial Pax Britannica which resulted in spreading death and destruction from the Cape to Cairo.

Moving to South Africa to head the Centre for Conflict Resolution (CCR) in Cape Town in 2003, I was shocked to discover the creation of the Mandela Rhodes Foundation in the same year as my arrival in the province where Cecil Rhodes had been prime minister for five years. The Rhodes Trust in Oxford contributed £10 million, in the first decade of the Mandela Rhodes Foundation, for African scholars to study at South African universities; to support child healthcare; and to provide sporting facilities for disadvantaged communities. But despite the positive impact that these funds have doubtless had, I persistently wondered about the wisdom of this monstrous marriage between the nineteenth century's greatest imperialist and one of the twentieth century's greatest moral figures. These are some of the issues that motivated me to write this book.

This work of creative non-fiction owes a debt of gratitude to four African literary ancestors. Set in an African "Hereafter" called After Africa, the novella is inspired by similar works by Kenya's Ali Mazrui's *The Trial of Christopher Okigbo* (1971), Zimbabwe's Stanlake Samkange's *On Trial For My Country* (1966), and Egyptian Naguib Mahfouz's short story *The Seventh Heaven* (2005): all political tales set in an imaginary after-life. South African author, Olive Schreiner's 1897 novella, *Trooper Peter Halket of Mashonaland*, which dealt with the excesses of Cecil Rhodes's marauding mercenaries in contemporary Zimbabwe, was also an important influence. I was further spurred on by legendary South African actors John Kani and Robert Whitehead's imaginative play *Congo: The Trial of King Leopold II*, which I saw at Johannesburg's Market Theatre in October 2018.

I would like, in closing, to express my gratitude to two external reviewers who took the time to provide extremely useful comments that helped to strengthen the work. I was enormously fortunate to have had three of South Africa's best editors working on the novella. Award-winning writer, Ken Barris, took the lead in smoothing out the rough edges. Russell Martin wielded his editorial pen as only a Cambridge-trained historian can, while Helen Moffett added stylistic flourishes to the early chapters. I would particularly like to thank Bridget Impey and Maggie Davies at Jacana Publishers who believed in this unusual project from the start, and supported it consistently until the very end. I would also like to thank my colleagues at the University of Johannesburg in South Africa and its Institute for Pan-African Thought and Conversation (IPATC) which I direct. Last but not least, it is important to acknowledge that I could not have travelled this journey without the great sacrifices of my mother, Adunni Adebajo.

Adekeye Adebajo
Johannesburg, November 2020

I

After Africa

7

II

The Counsel for
Damnation

77

III

The Counsel for
Salvation

113

IV

Judgment Day

141

I

After Africa

Cecil John Rhodes had been asleep. Still wearing a crumpled tweed jacket and white flannel trousers, he got to his feet slowly, and tried to look around, oppressed by the absolute darkness that surrounded him. He imagined vividly that he was in a tomb, with a colossal weight of stone above, threatening to bury him. He groped around until he stumbled painfully into a staircase that was as rough and cold to the touch as stone. He began to make his way upwards, feeling his way in the dark. He made a decision and began to grope his way. It was not long before light glowed dimly on the clammy walls, and then he heard distant screams that grew louder. Swift leathery shapes darted past his head, sending his heart racing – only bats, he tried to reassure himself.

Cecil turned a corner of the rocky winding stairway, and saw throngs of naked, wailing bodies being consumed by flames along the edges of a lake of fire that burnt with greater intensity than any flame he had ever seen before. The air stank of sulphur and brimstone, and the wailing grew louder. He saw shuddering bodies being eaten alive by rats and lizards, while figures with horns and hooves, darkly visible within the swarms of fiery serpents and dragons that swirled around them, poked burning spikes into the mass. Some had their skin flayed off their backs, and salt poured on their raw skin. Some had the soles of their feet dipped in burning sulphur. Others were disembowelled. The horned figures wielded a variety of torture implements: iron spikes, heated kettles, sharpened pangas and assegais, bloodied knobkerries. More frightening screams could be heard from condemned souls being skewered in a giant barbecue. Others were hoisted on spits and basted by taunting figures.

Creeping upwards, he recoiled in horror as he saw, without understanding how he knew what he saw, gluttons wallowing in filth amidst a hailstorm; carnal sinners being swept around by furious winds; traitors being cased in ice; the greedy endlessly stealing great stone weights from each other; spendthrifts torn apart by three-headed dogs; heretics burned in tombs; soothsayers condemned to walk backwards; hypocrites wandering aimlessly; adulterers tormented by a stream flowing with blood; alchemists struck with deadly plagues; suicides transformed into baobab and acacia trees; and flakes of fire raining down incessantly on the homicidal. Birds of prey gorged on raw flesh, even as a huge dragon with four large horns and blazing eyes was thrown into a lake of burning sulphur.

Cecil skirted the fringes of a more open space, in which even more hideous attention was given to a small number of victims. He could not know that among the most notable were Uganda's Idi Amin, whose regime had killed an estimated 300 000 people. Another was Emperor Jean-Bédél Bokassa of the Central African Republic who had squandered a quarter of his country's national income on a grandiloquent coronation. There was Nigeria's General Sani Abacha, the brutal ruler of Africa's most populous state, who infamously hanged eight environmental campaigners, and launched military operations that killed thousands of innocent people. Alongside were leaders of the genocidal militias in Rwanda who had killed 800 000 people in three months.

Cecil struggled past these horrific sights, climbing ever upwards, until light broke through at the end of the rocky steps. Reaching the top, he stumbled out gasping for air and bewildered. He lay down to catch his breath and did not know when he passed out, drifting into a deep slumber.

When he awoke, Cecil saw a forest in front of him, a dense swathe of green and yellow trees that stretched for miles. He climbed painfully to his feet, and began walking towards it. He spotted a long row of fever trees with green and yellow leaves, cracking bark and foliage in which roosted flocks of black hawks and brown and white eagles with yellow beaks nested. Towering above them were hundreds of ancient baobab trees with their gigantic trunks and slender tangled branches, on which vultures perched, alongside brown owls with glowing eyes. Mingled with them were vast numbers of mopane trees. He remembered the Shona word for them, meaning "butterfly," after the shape of its leaves which protect the tree from heat. He touched the tough termite-resistant mopane wood, and stared above at the green pigeons and green Cape weavers, which he also recognised.

Out of nowhere appeared a group of *Abiku*, child-ghosts who die in infancy and continue to be reborn with the same birthmarks. These ghost-children had a penchant for mischief, and this particular group followed Cecil through the forest chanting "*Oyinbo* pepper, leave the Bush of Ghosts! *Muzungu*, go back to England!" They tugged his clothing and leaped up to pull his hair, and trailed him singing the same tune. Frightened, Cecil broke into a run, and only left them behind when he exited the forest and staggered onto the muddy verge of a wide vlei (shallow lake), along which browsed flocks of sacred ibis, blue cranes, and brown and white storks with long orange beaks.

Eventually he passed around it and reached the other side, exhausted. He lay down to dry out his muddy clothes in the hot sun, wondering at the nature of this strange place. After a couple of hours, three bizarre human figures materialised, each covered in gold, silver, and bronze. One had no arms. The other hopped along on one leg, and the third had only one eye in the middle of her head. They did not speak, but beckoned him to follow them down a long trail through the grassland on the other side of the vlei, and into a large house. Inside, he was handed some Ethiopian *injera* bread and *wat* stew with assorted meats, which he devoured ravenously as the ghosts sat round a large marble table with him. He was also served West African palm wine from a brown gourd. As the friendly ghosts drifted to sleep, Cecil made for the door and escaped into the burning orange dusk. He walked as far as he could, until he lay down in a thicket of long grass as it was getting dark, and slept.

Cecil rose at first light, and walked on steadily, until he reached a large clear body of water shrouded in mist. He saw, floating clear of the mist, a hooded figure in a giant canoe. It reached the shore, and the ferryman grounded it. He stood up in the canoe, and approached. The ferryman pulled back the hood on his long black *djallaba* to reveal a mound of thick black hair, a handsome clean-shaven face, and glistening white teeth.

"I know you, Mr Rhodes. My name is Ahmed Ben Bella. You won't have heard of me. My task is to transport you across the lake, where a guide will take you on further."

He helped Cecil into the canoe, saw him seated, pushed the craft skilfully off the mud with his oar. Then he leaned forward and shook Cecil's hand.

"I was Algeria's founding head of state in the Herebefore, you know. I was instrumental in creating the Liberation Committee of the Organisation of African Unity at its inaugural summit in 1963, in Addis Ababa. Have you ever been there?"

Cecil shook his head.

"What liberation, you might be asking yourself, Mr Rhodes. It was nothing less than to complete the liberation of African countries from the various imperial powers that had oppressed us for so long."

A wave of shock passed through Cecil. What had happened while he slept?

"I famously implored my fellow leaders during the summit – yes, famously! – to let us agree to die a little or even completely, so that the peoples still under colonial domination might be free, and African unity might not be a vain word. The first part of my wish has now been fulfilled, but rather more literally than I intended at the time."

He picked up his oar, turned the craft away from the shore, and began to paddle.

The huge River Africa which Cecil and his ferryman proceeded to cross was made up of four large streams: the Nile, the Niger, the Congo, and the Zambezi, Africa's four greatest waterways. The flowing waters contained the tears of the multitude of sinners that Cecil had seen in the abyss out of which he had climbed. As Ben Bella paddled, Cecil sat terrified in the canoe, awed by the enormous river they were crossing with its violent turbulence that he was sure would tip the boat over.

Seeing Cecil's fear, the ferryman reached into his pocket, and passed him a can of cigarettes and a box of matches.

"Take it all," he said. "I'm trying to give up. They're Egyptian, you know."

Cecil thanked him, and lit one with some difficulty in the bouncing craft.

"Let me tell you a bit more about my background, Mr Rhodes. I actually fought for colonial France during the Second World War against Nazi Germany. I first fought in a French Alpine Infantry unit, in their defence against German air attacks – for which I won the *Croix de Guerre* – and subsequently was part of the Allied force that liberated Rome – for which I won the *Medaille Militaire.*

"I was thus a loyal subject of the Mother Country until radicalised by the French massacre of about 20 000 Algerian civilians. They attacked them from land, sea, and air in the cities of Setif, Guelma, and Kherrata. This happened on my return from service in Europe in May 1945. It was French General Charles de Gaulle himself who personally ordered these cowardly executions and lynchings of defenceless villagers. It was a response to the deaths of 102 *pieds-noirs,* European citizens born in Algeria. That in turn happened after the French army had killed thousands of peaceful Algerian demonstrators. Their crime? To demand their independence from recently liberated France."

Cecil was so tired that he struggled to follow. It was enough to relish his smoke.

"So many people were killed in this massacre that French soldiers dumped their bodies into ravines and wells. Even by France's sordid colonial record, this was one of the worst massacres in its history. It was on this day that I decided to join the Algerian national resistance, and became a founding member of the armed struggle in 1954.

"I survived two assassination attempts by French

security personnel two years later, before being imprisoned in France for the rest of the eight-year liberation war in which one million of my compatriots shed their blood to gain our freedom. I had been captured in 1956 after Paris treacherously forced my plane – having previously guaranteed safe passage – to be diverted to France, following a meeting with my liberation comrades in Rome. I was freed from jail at the end of the war, becoming the first president of Algeria. As earlier noted, I strongly supported Southern African liberation movements from Zimbabwe, South Africa, Angola, and Namibia, who were all given offices and training facilities in Algiers. We also contributed 100 million Francs to the OAU – that's the Organisation of African Unity – to their nine member Liberation Committee, of which Algeria was a founding member."

Cecil looked at him blankly.

"I can see you're exhausted," said the ferryman. "You can sleep over there, on that mattress. We're only going to get to the other side tomorrow morning."

Cecil seized this offer and soon fell into a deep sleep, despite the turbulence.

He awoke to a misty dawn morning, live with the call of birds. They had crossed the mighty river. As they approached the bank, Cecil sighted a figure waiting for them in the mist. It resolved into a woman of regal demeanour who waited for them to disembark, then held out her hand to greet Cecil and the ferryman. She was strikingly elegant, with proud brown eyes and high cheek bones. She was dressed in a garment made of beautiful red, orange, and green Ghanaian *kente* cloth with matching headgear, ornate ear-rings and a gold chain around her neck.

"Mr Rhodes, I presume? Welcome to After Africa. This is where all the departed souls from Africa and its diaspora end up. It is often said here that 'Death is an exercise in Pan-Africanism.' As the Kenyan political scientist Ali Mazrui noted, death is the most horizontal form of Pan-Africanism. My name is Efua Sutherland. I was from Ghana – the Gold Coast in your day – in the Herebefore, and have been in After Africa for about three decades. I have been assigned to be your guide. It is time for your trial in After Africa. But before this happens, I must first take you on a journey to five of After Africa's heavens. Your trial will take place in the fifth heaven, and there the decision will be made as to whether you can ascend to the sixth and seventh heavens."

Cecil was astonished by this revelation, but was not surprised that this woman knew his name. After some hesitation, he said, "It is a pleasure to meet you, Miss Sutherland, and thank you for—"

"Please call me Efua," interrupted the woman.

"I have wandered through the most terrifying scenes, first in a hellish underground cave, then in a forest and grassland full of dangers. Finally, I had to cross a vast perilous river in a canoe. What are all these places?"

"You have been dead for 120 years, Mr Rhodes, asleep in Limbo. You woke up in After Africa's Dungeon of Departed Souls, and wandered through the Bush of Ghosts, and crossed the River Africa. All new arrivals in our Hereafter experience this before their trial."

"What trial, and who presumes to judge me?"

His normally high voice cracked into an even higher falsetto whenever he was anxious or indignant. He was unused to being powerless, and it was a very uncomfortable experience.

"What will I be judged on during this trial, and who will be the judges? Will any of the judges be white?"

"What has this to do with the matter?"

"I fear my imperial achievements might not be impartially viewed by those who suffered their consequences," he responded drily.

"Anyone living in Africa beyond the grave can be a judge. In fact, we've had several white judges in the past. But you will have to be patient to discover their identity. You will have to wait to learn the nature of the crimes for which you will be tried. We have to wander through the four heavens before arriving at the fifth. Truth is revealed only slowly in After Africa, and much patience is required to discover its mysteries."

She took a hip flask from her bag, and handed it to him.

"It's Scotch," she said. "You'll probably need it."

There were many things that Cecil could not know. Among them was that Efua Sutherland had been a pioneer of African theatre during Ghana's heady post-independence days in the Herebefore. Using techniques such as traditional oratory and praise-poetry, she had sought to use theatre to liberate Africans from the trauma of five centuries of slavery and colonialism. She had created a drama studio in Accra for experimental theatre, interacting closely with the communities in which she worked to create an authentically indigenous theatre. Her *Kusum Agoromma* theatre group had travelled through many of Ghana's local communities, performing traditional theatre.

The artistic compound in which Efua had lived in the Herebefore had been named Araba Mansa (after her grandmother), and had become a site of pilgrimage for artists like Wole Soyinka from Nigeria, Kenya's Ngugi wa Thiong'o, Ghana's Ama Ata Aidoo, and the African American Maya Angelou. She had lived even her personal life as if she were playing it out on stage. Each festive season, she would construct a large hut with palm fronds, tinsel, and flowers and an outdoor bonfire around which her children would gather under the moonlight to hear traditional tales. Efua had famously prepared the body of one of the pioneers of contemporary Pan-Africanism, W.E.B. du Bois – who had lived out his last years in Ghana – for burial. This had created a close and enduring bond between them, which continued in After Africa.

The First Heaven:
The Historical Garden of the Ancestors

"We've reached the first heaven, Mr Rhodes."

Cecil made no reply. Instead he reached for the tin of Egyptian cigarettes in his shirt pocket, took one out and lit it to cover his nervousness.

A thin, distinguished man approached them. Despite his anxiety, Rhodes noted with approval the dark blue flowing *boubou* that nearly reached the ground, with an embroidered, matching blue hat. No doubt, he thought ironically, a sophisticated "savage."

"Good morning. I am Sundiata, originally from Mali. We are the fabled griots who pass on the history of our people to successive generations. I will show you around this first heaven, narrating a brief history of Africa's ancient glories in the Historical Garden of the Ancestors."

Sundiata led them through two stately pillars that stretched into the clouds, into a giant park with lush green grass and throngs of exquisitely colourful flowers. Ornate, round brown calabashes were also scattered all over the vast estate that stretched endlessly, seemingly into eternity, and they walked in the bright sunshine.

"As you know," said the griot, "Africa was the birthplace of humanity. It is the site of the original

Garden of Eden, which was located in East Africa near the Rift Valley."

Cecil knew no such thing, but limited himself to raising an eyebrow.

"To our left is the prototypal garden, with a winged angel who guards the entrance, carrying a flaming sword. In the middle of this forest is the Tree of Life – over there, to the left – as you can see, it is a baobab. To the right – there it is – you see the Tree of the Knowledge of Good and Evil. It is an acacia tree."

A giant black panther coiled itself around the trunk of the legendary acacia. There was something odd, strangely repulsive, about its movements. Cecil peered at it more closely, then recoiled in horror as he saw that it was crawling upside down.

"Don't be afraid, said Sundiata, chuckling gently. "That is the Satanic serpent but it will not do you any harm as it is cursed to remain in the garden for eternity. Its punishment for introducing Death into the world."

The griot launched into his brief history of Africa, "I will take you through a history of some of the continent's greatest empires all the way to the European conquest of the continent, accomplished – as you will know, your role in it was not inconsiderable – by the late nineteenth century."

He gestured at a tableau: "To our left is Egypt's

Sphinx with her human head and lion's body guarding the famous pyramids at Giza. Egypt was unified into one entity by Pharaoh Mentuhotep II between 2041 and 2016 BCE. Do you realise, Mr Rhodes, that he achieved this nearly 4 000 years before Otto von Bismarck unified Germany's feuding city-states?

"There was – as you can see – an advanced irrigation system with pyramids, temples, canals, and a complex tax-collection system. Trade extended as far as the Levant, the Red Sea, and the Mediterranean. They used horse-drawn chariots and bronze weapons during this period, the giant replicas which you can see before you. It was in 332 BCE that Alexander the Great conquered Egypt, introducing the Ptolemaic dynasty. They didn't last long, less than 300 years. Then the Ptolemaic dynasty ended with Roman rule in 30 BC."

Cecil stood astounded, observing this lost city of ancient Africa with amazement.

Sundiata walked on at a steady pace, stopping at another tableau and turning to his guests.

"Here are the famous ruins of Carthage. Today it would be in Tunisia. Carthage had become a major trading power in the Mediterranean by 600 BCE, resulting in the emergence of the Berber kingdoms. They traded in gold, ivory, beads, and slaves." Sensing Rhodes's amazement, Sundiata noted: "Yes,

Mr Rhodes, some ancient Africans were slavers too, as well as your own kind. The Carthaginians were eventually defeated in the three Punic Wars with Rome, between 264 and 146 BCE. It resulted in the birth of the Roman province of Africa, which became a major supplier of agricultural goods for the empire. The Berber civilization eventually came to dominate Carthage after 420 AD, when Rome's power declined."

Sundiata moved forward purposefully, stopping at a giant Aksumite obelisk and gesticulating: "This is from the Aksum Empire, which by the fifth century BCE was one of the world's most prosperous regions. They manufactured copper, brass, and glass crystals, which you can see next to the obelisk. You can also see the gold and silver coins that were minted in ancient Aksum. This kingdom stretched through contemporary Sudan, Ethiopia, and Eritrea in the Herebefore. You can also see the stone palaces and megalithic monuments under which the kings of Aksum were buried."

The trio continued their walk in the shade of the huge tree-lined park in glorious sunshine relieved by cool shadow. At their next stop, Sundiata resumed his narration: "The Sao civilisation reached its zenith in the sixth century BCE, and survived until the sixteenth century AD in Central Africa. You can see the iron, copper, and bronze artefacts of its skilled artisans. Next to them are original examples of the jewellery, pottery, and spears produced by this ancient civilisation. An estimated 90 percent of this art was looted by European colonizers, and are now, beyond the grave, in museums in London, Paris, Brussels, Lisbon, and Berlin. Beside this is the Kanem Empire which flourished from the ninth century AD until 1893. It was a major player in the trans-Saharan trade with its famous caravans and sordid commerce in human chattel, all of which are replicated here. This large life-size army here, next to the caravans, symbolise the 40 000-strong cavalry that the empire was able to field in the thirteenth century."

Cecil opened his mouth in amazement. "I had no idea," he whispered to Efua, "of this rich African history." He had thought that Africa's history began only with the arrival of Europeans, but couldn't admit it to her. He could hardly face the realisation himself.

Sundiata overheard this comment, but chose not to respond. Instead he walked on, pointing to the Bornu Empire which he noted had traded in gold, horses, and salt, and had also imported firearms by the sixteenth century, establishing diplomatic links with the Ottoman Empire. Next was the Kongo Empire of the fifteenth century which the griot noted had produced scores of artisans in pottery, weaving, and metalwork, while establishing a regional trading network.

Sundiata moved briskly to the Sultanate of Mogadishu, pointing to a giant-size replica of the famous Almnara Tower, before explaining that ships had come to Mogadishu from as far away as Arabia, India, Venice, Portugal, Persia, and China. He noted that Somali traders had exported zebras, giraffes, and incense to Ming China. The loquacious griot then pointed out huge replicas of palaces and four-story buildings that Portuguese explorer, Vasco da Gama, had described with approval in the fifteenth century.

Sundiata walked further into this giant Jurassic park of African history. He stopped at an information board describing the origins of the ironworks of the Zulus dating from the eleventh century. He then pointed to the spectacular stone Towers of Great Zimbabwe which Cecil knew of. He had declared that it had been built by some bastard race, with white blood flowing through its veins. It was obvious that no African could have conceived of such a magnificent structure. But now he was being forced to think differently by everything he had seen here. Sundiata went on to describe in detail the gold, copper, and ivory of the Mapungubwe kingdom of the twelfth century CE. The griot explained to an incredulous Cecil that this had been a black African empire, with Great Zimbabwe being the first city in Southern Africa.

Noticing that his guests were becoming fatigued, Sundiata reassured them, "Our last stop will be the West African empires, and I will try to speed up here. First up is the Ghana empire from the eight century AD, which made its wealth from the Trans-Saharan trade and also controlled goldfields, giant replicas of which you can see here. Next to that is the Mali Empire from the thirteenth century. My namesake, King Sundiata of the Mandingos, conquered much territory for this empire, based on its gold and salt trade. He further used a competent administrative system to secure his kingdom. King Musa's famous fourteenth century *hajj* to Mecca is also captured here, with a magnificent replica of his famous 500 gold-carrying slaves. This incident dropped the global price of gold for a decade. Malian kings further established two of the world's greatest centres of Islamic learning in Timbuktu and Djenné, established centuries before much of Europe had created many of its famous universities."

Cecil was amazed to learn about these educational institutions, asking the griot incredulously whether these had really existed. Sundiata answered affirmatively, noting that some of Timbuktu's manuscripts had been preserved in historic time too.

"Next is the Songhai Empire from the ninth century," continued the griot, "with a replica of its army, complete with cavalry and canoes. Moving along, we have the Akan kingdom dating back to the twelfth century, based on gold wealth and a formidable, all-conquering army. The Asante Empire anticipated a more recent outlook by centuries – they had a matrilineal royal family."

Cecil didn't know what he meant by that – his own Queen Victoria in England had of course been a woman, but the throne wasn't matrilineal – but he was too overwhelmed to say anything.

Sundiata then stepped up the pace before pausing in front of the replica of an all-female fighting unit. "This is an Amazonian unit in the army of Dahomey," he said. "In the seventeenth century it was a powerful, well organised kingdom that traded with European merchants.

"Next up is the famous Oyo Empire, home of the Yorubas of southwest Nigeria. Oyo conquered Dahomey. It developed a complex system of city-states with the Ooni of Ife at its head. Other kings – they were called *obas* – became autonomous, with the Alafin of Ibadan developing a cavalry force to challenge Ife's hegemony.

"The Oyo Empire had great artisans who made cloth, pottery, and ironware. Next to Oyo is the Benin kingdom from the fifteenth century, where the King ruled through an advisory council called the *uzama* to ensure checks and balances in monarchical decision-making. Benin traded with the Portuguese and Dutch, and you can see an original of the famous Benin bronze in front of you."

Cecil stared at the ornate bronze artefact in disbelief, as Efua ran her hand along its surface to feel the texture.

Sundaiata walked on, then stopped abruptly at the edge of the exit of the giant park which also had two large pillars reaching to the clear white clouds, each resembling the biblical Tower of Babel. "So, we have reached the end of our tour of the Historical Garden of the Ancestors. The last point I just wanted to make – which may be relevant to Mr Rhodes's forthcoming trial – is that, while only ten percent of Africa had been colonised in 1880, within three decades, ninety percent of the entire continent had come under European colonial rule. As I mentioned before, Mr Rhodes, you played a not too insignificant role in this conquest. Thank you, thank you for your earnest attention."

Rhodes turned bright red and fidgeted in his pockets to find the flask of Scotch whisky. He took a generous swig before returning it to his pocket. He was sweating profusely, and used a white handkerchief to wipe his brow. He simultaneously felt a strange mixture of apprehension at his impending trial. Also a twist, soon buried, of admiration for the rich history of ancient Africa that he had just experienced.

The Second Heaven:
The Guild of Nobel Laureates

As they ended their tour of the first heaven, and Sundiata bade them farewell, Cecil and Efua ascended some hills, before coming upon a gathering seated around a table, consuming biltong and peanuts. Efua explained to Cecil that they had reached the second heaven, known as the Guild of Nobel Laureates.

"Nobel Laureates?" he asked.

"Winners of the Nobel Prize: the most prestigious awards beyond the grave."

"Anything to do with the Nordic explosives magnate, Alfred Nobel?"

"Yes, exactly."

"Never met him, though I was into explosives myself. He was thought to be a capable fellow."

Two men sat in comfortable armchairs in front of which was a table full of tea, coffee, cakes, and sandwiches. Ralph Bunche was a tall, handsome, Harvard-trained African American, and former scholar-diplomat, wearing a smartly tailored dark suit. He was in deep conversation with Chief Albert Luthuli, who wore on top of a dark blue suit a leopard skin hat and a necklace of lion's teeth. Luthuli was promoting Christian principles, notably learning to turn the other cheek and to forgive one's opponents.

Bunche was sceptical. "My mediation efforts in the Middle East with the United Nations taught me that these principles cannot work in practice, and in my experience Old Testament values, an eye for an eye, were the prevalent norms and values of this region."

As they continued their friendly argument, Efua explained to an intrigued Cecil that Bunche was the first black person to win the Nobel Peace Prize.

"His skilful intervention in the Middle East earned him the award. Bunche served the United Nations for another two decades, contributing to global peacemaking efforts in the Suez and Congo crises of the twentieth century."

"The man he is conversing with was the second black man after Bunche to win the Nobel Peace Prize, Chief Albert Luthuli. He headed what was to become South Africa's foremost liberation party, the African National Congress. The Nobel prize came shortly after the Sharpeville massacre in South Africa in 1960, and was an attempt to highlight apartheid's brutalities. Luthuli is known in After Africa as the 'Black Moses' having titled his autobiography *Let My People Go*. It was taken from a civil rights era American Negro spiritual often heard in After Africa."

What civil rights era? wondered Rhodes. Perhaps Efua was referring to the Pax Victoriana. After all, he had never felt any shortage of civil rights, and there were even a few Indian boys down at Oxford.

Before he could ask, Efua broke into a soft song:

"Go down, Moses, way down in Egypt's land

Tell old Pharaoh to let my people go!"

She glanced at him sharply and continued, "For Luthuli, who was deeply steeped in Christian religious beliefs, the road to freedom lay through the cross. Sacrifices and suffering would be required in order to translate Jesus Christ's ethic of love into concrete achievements. The cross thus had to come before the crown. The point of the struggle for him was to transform the enemy's hatred through love and human dignity. These are still among the predominant values of After Africa."

As they walked further, they spotted four men and a woman seated calmly under the shade of a marula tree on the grass in a beautiful garden with bowls of fruits – mangoes, guavas, and pineapples – lined up around a wooden table in front of them. On one side was Martin Luther King Jr, a tall and handsome man dressed casually in jeans and a long white shirt. Beside him sat Anwar Sadat dressed in a white long, simple *djallaba* in honour of his peasant roots, smoking a brown pipe. On the other side of a wooden table was the exuberant Wangari

Maathai, dressed in a loose-fitting blue and white cotton African traditional dress that reached the ground. Next to her was the imposing figure of Nelson Mandela dressed in jeans and a multi-coloured African shirt. Beside him was the soft-spoken Kofi Annan, dressed casually in jeans and a black polo shirt. They were animatedly playing a board game called Making Earthly Peace. Each team took turns to roll two white-and-black dice, following which they moved chess-like figures across conflict zones and ganglands with names such as Somalia, Sudan, Central African Republic, Mali, Chicago, Los Angeles, Kingston, and Port of Spain. Maathai patted Mandela and Annan excitedly on the back, as their team appeared to be doing better than King and Sadat, who kept throwing their arms up in exasperation.

"These are Africa's five Nobel Peace laureates," explained Efua. "Martin Luther King Jr was the martyred American civil rights leader who became the youngest winner of the Nobel Peace Prize at the age of only 35. King was murdered only four years after winning the Nobel Peace Prize, and is widely acknowledged here to be one of the most eloquent orators to have entered the realm of the ancestors."

She pointed to Sadat. "Egyptian leader Anwar Sadat was assassinated by religious extremists with help from elements in his own army, having won the

Peace Prize following his historic trip to Jerusalem, and making peace with Israel. You might remember it as Palestine, a small part of the Ottoman Empire that later fell under Jewish control."

Efua turned to the others, without waiting for his response.

"Nelson Mandela is a fairly recent arrival in After Africa. He spent 27 years in jail fighting for his beliefs before creating a democratic South Africa as the country's first president. His entry into the Hereafter was joyously celebrated! Playing alongside him is Kenya's Wangari Maathai. She unexpectedly won the Nobel Peace Prize for her environmental and civil rights activism across East Africa. Up until then, only conventional peace activists had won the award. Next to her is my compatriot in the Herebefore, Kofi Annan, who won the Nobel Peace Prize while serving as United Nations Secretary-General for a decade."

Cecil was bewildered by all these people and institutions that he'd never heard of, but didn't wish to keep interrupting her with questions.

As Efua and Cecil went further, they noticed in the same garden a circle of people deep in conversation.

"They're writers,'" explained Efua. "The one wearing a light brown suit with the square dark glasses smoking a hookah is Egypt's Naguib Mahfouz. He wrote 34 novels and was the first Arab writer to win the Nobel Prize for Literature. He loved to sit in cafés in Cairo observing the actions of ordinary people, which had inspired him to develop many of his colourful fictional characters. His habit of writing the truth as he saw it almost cost him his life."

"How so?"

"His allegory, *Children of the Gebelawi*, raised fundamental questions about religious beliefs and the rise of the three monotheistic faiths: Islam, Christianity, and Judaism. The book was dismissed by religious zealots as heretical, and Mahfouz only narrowly survived a stabbing, which nearly saw him joining us here earlier than his arrival. He was so terrified of flying that he sent his two daughters to Stockholm to receive the Nobel prize on his behalf."

She pointed to a woman seated next to Mahfouz. "That is the Zimbabwean-British writer, Doris Lessing." She wore a long black skirt, a blue and red shirt, and a simple black necklace. She had neatly packed grey hair and puffy red cheeks.

"What do you mean by 'Zimbabwean'? It's just a long-abandoned fortress," interjected Rhodes. "No-one comes from there."

"It is now the land that was once called Southern Rhodesia."

Cecil blanched. "God spare us," he muttered under his breath.

Efua seemed not to notice.

"Lessing became the oldest Nobel literature laureate at the age of 88. Then she arrived here six years later."

Lessing looked animated, as she chatted away with two other women.

"Those two are Nadine Gordimer and Toni Morrison on her right."

Nadine Gordimer wore a white shirt covered with a black and orange silk scarf, and had her hand on her chin in a reflexive pose. Next to her was the silver-haired dreadlocked Toni Morrison in a brown polo short and white necklace.

"South Africa's Nadine Gordimer was a Nobel literature laureate who wrote ten novels and published prolifically on apartheid crimes in her racist country and other social issues relating to post-independence Africa. Her novel *July's People* remains one of the most important books in the Herebefore. Next to her is African American Toni Morrison, also a Nobel literature laureate. She is a more recent arrival in After Africa. She wrote eleven novels, with *Beloved* being her *magnum opus*. This tragic tale of infanticide was based on a true incident. An escaped nineteenth century slave woman in America's pre-bellum South slit her daughter's throat when recaptured, so that the child would not have to live in slavery."

Cecil recoiled in horror at hearing this tale, and

stared at its writer for a few minutes before both continued walking further.

"Well," he said doggedly, "the British Empire abolished slavery twenty years before I was born."

"But the British government perversely compensated the slave-owners for ending slavery at the cost of £200 billion in today's money beyond the grave. The legacy of slavery continues today in Africa and the diaspora in the Herebefore, while reparations have still not been paid to its tens of millions of victims and their descendants," she replied. A startled Cecil had no response to this sharp retort.

They next encountered two men sitting across from each other. One was an earnest-looking black man with brown-rimmed glasses and a receding hair-line in a smart white shirt and brown corduroy trousers. The other brown-skinned man had a mop of black curly hair and a black moustache and was also casually dressed in jeans and a colourful Arab shirt. They sat under a sycamore tree, with the black man reading a large door-stopper of a book on economic theory. The brown-skinned man was reading an equally cumbersome book on science. Efua greeted the men who looked up briefly to wave to her, before continuing their reading. She turned to Cecil. "The man in the glasses is a Fabian intellectual from St Lucia, Arthur Lewis, who won the Nobel Prize for Economics."

Cecil was shocked. "Did a black man really win the Nobel Prize for Economics?" he asked Efua incredulously.

She nodded, and continued, "Lewis served as economic adviser to my president, *Osagyefo* – that means 'Redeemer' – Kwame Nkrumah, who is, of course, also here with us in After Africa. The Caribbean economist won the Nobel prize for the 'dual sector' or 'Lewis model' which argued that a capitalist sector develops by moving labour from a subsistence sector which has an unlimited supply of workers. As a result, wages can be kept low. The higher returns are then reinvested in capital accumulation, expanding employment by drawing more workers from the subsistence sector, resulting in self-sustaining economic development and eventually modernization."

Cecil nodded several times, following the flow of the argument.

"China's incredible unprecedented lifting of 500 million people out of poverty in the Herebefore borrowed from many of Lewis's ideas," Efua continued.

Cecil stood stunned by these revelations, and kept staring in disbelief at the bespectacled Lewis. He finally exclaimed to Efua, "I really did not realise that a black thinker could have had such a massive impact on the theory and practice of economics."

Efua then pointed to the scientist. "That is Egypt's Ahmed Zewail who won the Nobel prize for chemistry for using laser technology to produce flashes of light. He is widely known as the originator of femtochemistry and is a fairly recent arrival in After Africa. I won't try to explain these scientific developments to you now, but they were, and remain, extremely advanced."

"You can hardly say he was African, can you? The man's obviously an Egyptian!"

"And on what continent is Egypt?"

Despite himself, Rhodes was disturbed, even agitated. He couldn't think of a reply, knowing full well that he looked down on Egyptians too, regardless of their continent.

"There are even more African Nobel laureates, Cecil: Nigerian Wole Soyinka and South African John M. Coetzee both won the prize for literature, while South Africa's Desmond Tutu and F.W. De Klerk, Egypt's Mohamed El-Baradei, and Liberians Ellen Johnson-Sirleaf and Leymah Gbowee won the award for peace.

Cecil looked away, struggling to digest this information, struggling to understand why it disturbed him so much.

Efua tapped him on the shoulder and suggested that they continue on their journey.

The Third Heaven:
Dead Poets' Society

Efua and Cecil ascended another range of hills, after which Efua announced that they were now entering After Africa's third heaven. "This place is known as the Dead Poets' Society, since it showcases Africa's writing achievements beyond the grave," she explained.

At the entrance, Efua greeted Nigerian novelist Chinua Achebe, who had fairly recently arrived in After Africa. As the grey-haired, red-capped, bespectacled Achebe wandered away, Efua told Cecil about him.

"Chinua has been described as the father of the contemporary African novel. His 1958 classic, *Things Fall Apart,* sold 12 million copies and was translated into over 50 languages, making him the continent's most widely read novelist. A member of Nigeria's large Igbo ethnic group, he introduced his people's culture and cosmology to the world through simple prose based on local folklore and oral traditions rich with proverbs. He was the most prominent of the Heinemann African writers' series, which developed an African literary canon of 273 novels, publishing many of the writers whom you will see shortly."

Cecil was – he had to admit it now – surprised and impressed. Such a thing was unknown in his lifetime.

"Achebe's early novels dealt with the personal tragedies that arose from the clash of cultures between African tradition and intrusive Western values imported by colonial mandarins and missionaries. His later novels and essays provided devastating critiques of a corpulent and corrupt Nigerian political class that had squandered its bountiful inheritance. Achebe was equally unsparing of Nigerian citizens whom he felt condoned the excesses of their leaders. He was so disgusted with the parlous state of his homeland, that he twice rejected a prestigious national award."

Efua took a moment to drink some water from a gourd at her waist, and Cecil again took a swig from his flask of Scotch.

"Achebe consistently challenged European narratives of Africa for dehumanising its people and denying them their own history. His work was as important for the living, as it is for us here. 'Until the lions produce their own historian,' he once said, 'the story of the hunt will glorify only the hunter.' In Achebe's celebrated critique of Joseph Conrad's *Heart of Darkness* which I am sure you knew, he described the Polish Englishman as a 'purveyor of comforting myths' and a 'thoroughgoing racist,' whose work is 'a story in which the very humanity of black people is called in question.'"

Cecil had never heard of Conrad. For all he knew, the man could have been a literary jingoist, a species of which he had once approved. But by now, he was growing deeply uncomfortable, understanding that his views were out of kilter with the prevailing values of this strange new world.

There was a group of writers in shining white togas in earnest discussion with Chinua Achebe, seated around a table piled with roast turkey, jollof rice, and *couscous*. Efua briefly explained who they were. The smartly dressed man in a white shirt and tweed jacket was South Africa's Sol Plaatje who had written *Mhudi*. The first published novel in English by an African; next to him was Lesotho's Thomas Mofolo, who had written the novel *Chaka* in Sesotho. Both were in animated discussion with the Afro-Trinidadian, C.L.R. James, author of *The Black Jacobins,* an account of the eighteenth century Haitian slave revolt. Nigerian novelist, Amos Tutuola, who had written the famous *Palm-Wine Drinkard,* African American Ralph Ellison who had published *Invisible Man,* and Guinea's Camara Laye who had written the enchanting *The African Child,* were all in their own circle. The great African American writer and essayist, James Baldwin, with his large, bulging eyes, was in a deep conversation with South African writer-activist Alex la Guma who, Efua explained, had faced constant detentions and bans from the racist apartheid regime in South Africa for his activism. He was the author of *A Walk in the Night*, a classic which had vividly captured the horrific violence and dehumanisation of his homeland.

Efua had used this term "apartheid" a number of times. At last Rhodes asked her what it was, and so she tried to explain. A dogmatic and humourless people, the Afrikaners, he thought. It didn't seem much unlike the dispensation in his own time, though perhaps it was unnecessarily systematic. At worst, the Calvinist Boers stood to be accused of rigidity, unreasonableness, and political naivete.

But then he felt a sudden panic, realising how starkly the axis of the world had tilted.

"I'm no longer a worldly man," he said out loud, hoarsely. "I'm an infant here." He faltered before he could add, "out of my depth."

Efua gazed at him impassively, and then walked on.

As they proceeded, they passed another table where a quartet of women clad in multi-coloured African prints were gathered around a wide basket of oranges, bananas, and apples.

"That is Kenya's first female playwright, Rebeka Njau, whose *Ripples in the Pool* had innovatively explored the tale of a high-class city prostitute who was driven to insanity and murder by her claustrophobic, chauvinistic society. Beside her is Bessie Head, a South African who lived and worked in exile in Botswana. She wrote ten novels dealing with issues of mental illness and patriarchy. Next to her is the Indian-South African scholar-activist, Fatima Meer, who wrote biographies of Mahatma Gandhi and Nelson Mandela whom you encountered earlier in the second heaven; and at the end is the Senegalese writer Mariama Bâ, whose poignant *So Long A Letter* dealt with the difficult issues of polygamy and patriarchy in a Muslim community."

Efua told Cecil that Bâ had entered After Africa at the age of only 52. She added that Bessie Head had little tolerance for patronising and racist behaviour, and had supreme self-belief.

"She died even younger at the age of 49, arriving in After Africa earlier than expected."

Efua warmly embraced each of the four female writers; she was clearly close friends with them.

Further along the table were other writers. Efua once again described each to Cecil.

"That is Egyptian playwright, Tewfik al-Hakim, whose famous collection of plays *The Fate of A Cockroach* elicited comparisons with Romanian playwright, Eugéne Ionesco; next to him is Robert Serumaga of Uganda, author of the *Return of the Shadows*. He was lucky to escape being incarcerated by the thugs of dictator Idi Amin whom you would have encountered in the Dungeon of Departed Souls at the beginning of your journey. He later became his country's minister of commerce before dying at 41, and arriving prematurely in After Africa. Next to him is Ethiopia's Daniachew Worku whose novel, *The Thirteenth Sun*, explored an ultimately fatal pilgrimage of a sick father and son to the shrine of Addo in the Ethiopian mountains. Seated next to him is Tayeb Salih whose haunting novel, *Season of Migration to the North*, was described by the Palestinian-American writer Edward Said as 'one of the six most important works of Arab fiction.' It was translated into no fewer than 20 languages. Next to him is Morocco's Driss Chraibi, author of *Heirs to the Past*."

Sitting alone brooding in the corner was the Zimbabwean *enfant terrible*, Dambudzo Marechera. Efua explained that Marechera was a writer of great potential who was expelled from Oxford University for reportedly trying to burn down his college.

"His haunting novel, *The House of Hunger* won widespread acclaim, but he died young at the age of 35. His entry into After Africa was so unexpected that he was forced to spend three decades in Limbo before his trial beyond the grave for his reckless acts."

Efua and Cecil then approached a group of writers seated around a fire reciting poetry. At the centre of this group were two pioneers of the Negritude school of poetry: Martinique's Aimé Césaire and Senegal's poet-president Léopold Senghor. Alongside them were the Martinican René Maran, whom Efua explained was the first black man to win France's top literary prize – the Prix Goncourt – for his fiery novel *Batouala*; and Nigerian literary critic, Abiola Irele who had recently arrived in After Africa. Seated next to them was Edward Blyden of the Caribbean island of St Thomas, a scholar-statesman, widely regarded as the intellectual father of Pan-Africanism, and a major influence on the Negritude School.

"These apostles of Negritude glorified black culture, looked back nostalgically at a rich African past, and affirmed the worth and dignity of black people across the globe."

As Efua and Cecil watched, Césaire rose and recited one of his famous poems:

My Negritude is not a stone, its deafness thrown
    against the
Clamour of the day
My Negritude is not a film of dead water on the
    dead eye of
The day....
My Negritude is no tower and no cathedral
It delves into the deeper red flesh of the soil...

Léopold Senghor next stepped forward, and read from some of his own poems:

> *Naked woman, black woman*
> *I sing your passing beauty and fix it for all*
> *Eternity*
> *Before jealous Fate reduces you to ashes to nourish*
> *the roots of life...*
>
> *They call us men of cotton, coffee, and oil*
> *They call us men of death*
> *But we are men of dance, whose feet draw strength*
> *As we pound upon firm ground...*
>
> *Lord God, forgive white Europe!*
> *It's true, Lord, that for centuries of*
> *Enlightenment she threw her foaming,*
> *Yelping dogs upon my lands...*

Cecil cringed at the powerful words of this last poem. Efua then whispered to him that in the Herebefore, Césaire had turned a Western classic into a parable of the Western exploitation of Africa and its diaspora.

"Set in the Caribbean, Césaire's play, *Une Tempête,* adapted Shakespeare's *The Tempest* to portray a European Prospero enslaving a black Caliban. Shakespeare's Caliban is a primitive half-beast, half-man creature, reported to have been fathered by a devil and a witch, and been banished from Algiers to a deserted island. Prospero treats Caliban harshly, enslaving and tormenting him. Césaire's Caliban – unlike Shakespeare's – however eventually rebels against Prospero."

Cecil shivered as he listened to this tale, and lit up yet another cigarette, his hands visibly trembling.

Also present in another circle nearby was Phyllis Wheatley whom Efua explained had been a former slave from West Africa in the eighteenth century who grew up in a white Boston family in the US, becoming the first black woman to publish a book of poetry, which had sought to promote a more positive image of Africa and was widely read. Next to her was another poet-president, Angola's Agostinho Neto whose poems had often been used in the Herebefore as popular political songs during his country's struggle to be liberated from Portuguese rule. Here too was Senegalese-Cameroonian poet, David Diop, whose *Coups de Pilon* had been published to much acclaim. Diop had arrived early in After Africa following a plane crash, aged only 33. Next to him was another poet who had died young. Nigeria's Christopher Okigbo was killed at the age of 35 by his country's federal army during Nigeria's civil war. Okigbo fought at the rank of major for the unsuccessful Biafran secessionists, having abandoned his pen for the pistol.

The Nigerian poet, whose slight frame belied his supreme self-confidence, then got up to recite one of his poems:

Watchman for the watchword
At Heavensgate;

out of the depths my cry;
Give ear and hearken...

The stars have departed,
The sky in monocle
Surveys the world under.

The stars have departed
And I – where am I?

The Fourth Heaven:
The Celestial Music Concert

Cecil and his guide departed the third heaven with this lyrical poetry still ringing in their ears. They plodded along slowly to the top of another range of mountainous hills. Just below them was a large amphitheatre, to which they climbed down and entered. A giant stage was framed by a dazzling set of lights, and hundreds of thousands of After Africa's inhabitants waited in anticipation for the celestial musical concert that was to take place in the fourth heaven.

First to be introduced was Ghana's E.T. Mensah, a leading figure in Africa's dance-band highlife of the 1950s. He wore a black cap and carried a saxophone. He was accompanied by the Ghanaian King Bruce and Nigerian Victor Olaiya, Bobby Benson and Rex Lawson who played the drums, talking drums and trumpet. The group blasted hit after hit from the *Highlife Giants* album on which Mensah and Olaiya had collaborated. The audience danced to the swing and jazz rhythms and Afro-Cuban and calypso percussions of the band, breaking into rapturous applause at the end of the set.

"My country before the grave, Ghana," Efua explained, "introduced highlife music combining *osibisa Fante* rhythms with brass band music brought to Ghana by West Indian colonial soldiers, Liberian guitar music imported by Kru sailors, and *asiko* and *gombe* brought from Sierra Leone by freed Maroon slaves from Jamaica in the early nineteenth century. You can see that our music is very cosmopolitan. The great Mensah was given a state funeral when he died, the same year that I myself arrived in After Africa."

Next to appear on stage were the Congolese musicians of the African belle époque of the 1950s and 1960s: Joseph Le Grand Kalle Kabasele and his African Jazz colleagues, including guitar wizard Nicholas Dr Nico Kasanda. Also joining them was the legendary Franco Luambo Makiadi of the prominent group of the era, OK Jazz. The musicians launched into the 1960 hit "Independence Cha Cha Cha," which celebrated the end of Belgian colonial rule. It became an anthem across much of Africa, with 17 countries gaining their independence in that annus mirabilis. African and Latin rumba rhythms rang out across the large amphitheatre as the citizens of After Africa broke into spontaneous dance, doing the subtle hip movements associated with that fabled music.

Then, Fela Anikulapo ("he who carries death in his pouch") Kuti, the Nigerian superstar known for his radical political stance and bohemian lifestyle – he smoked marijuana, wore underwear on camera, married 27 wives, and arrived in After Africa at the age of 58, having succumbed to AIDS – emerged from the back of the stage with his saxophone hanging from his neck, amidst rapturous applause and cries of "Baba 70" and "Abami Eda, which means "the weird one". The man with the perpetually youthful face, furrowed brows and large brown eyes was wearing an embroidered blue, yellow, and red outfit.

Efua, swinging from side to side to the rhythmic beats, turned to Cecil, "Fela was not only a musical Orpheus who made magic with his saxophone; he was a political Cassandra whose prophecies often went unheeded by cynical and sceptical Africans, with the conservative middle-classes often dismissing him as a decadent, half-naked, marijuana-smoking madman, a soulful Socrates of counter-culture who corrupted Africa's youth and led them astray.

"He bucked the trend to develop his own unique fusion of African indigenous rhythms and jazz. Fela used his native Yoruba language and pidgin English to reach a mass audience, and spoke for the voiceless and powerless. A man of the people, he sang about social issues and everyday life that ordinary people could relate to.

"He mocked the materialism of African women; ridiculed the false bravado of Nigerian men which Fela called *shakara*; and lambasted the continent's political class as 'beasts of no nations' for selling out their countries and mortgaging their children's future.

"For Fela, redemption was to be sought on earth and not in some nebulous Hereafter. Paradise was to be achieved not through passive fatalism, but through revolutionary thought and action. But here he is entertaining us in After Africa."

The stage was set up like the Shrine, Fela's commune of debauchery in the sweltering Nigerian city of Lagos before the grave. The beat of African drums and percussion was accompanied by Fela on the keyboard, even as electric guitars matched the rhythms. The flamboyant bandmaster conducted the orchestra with great aplomb. Flashing a gap-toothed smile at the audience, he screamed, "Everybody say yeah, yeah!" which the huge audience screamed back as one. Pacing up and down with his characteristic stalking dance, Fela then started singing about a long, long time ago when English colonialists came to Africa on their imperial missions. As he noted, "Where you take our land by force, there must be Englishman."

Cecil's face darkened with shame.

Fela continued to wave his hands around frantically, took off his shirt, and launched into a solo on his huge saxophone to rapturous cheers from the After Africa multitude. On stage with Fela were 15 of his Dancing Queens, with their faces painted white, wearing long braids and heavy orange beads around their necks, rings on their fingers, copper bracelets and large ear rings. They joined Fela in his choruses and got on their knees, provocatively thrusting their hips. Half of them wore traditional *ankara* dresses of vivid yellow, while the other half wore dark blue.

In a final spectacular scene, a melancholy Fela was seen apparently hallucinating like a Black Hamlet in a haze of smoke, while using African masquerades – ancestral masked dancers – as intermediaries to visit his mother in the land of the ancestors in the spectacular dance of the deities. The Afro-beat superstar then raised both arms in his characteristic sign of defiant triumph, and left the stage to thunderous applause.

Next on stage was Bob Marley.

"Like Fela," explained Efua, "the Jamaican reggae superstar was a musical genius and prophet of Pan-Africanism. He spread the gospel of Rastafarianism across the world. He arrived in After Africa at the age of only 36, having succumbed to cancer. His astonishing legacy is confirmed by the fact that his music, involving about 20 albums, still accounts for half of all reggae music sold in the Herebefore. He was probably the most famous and recognisable individual ever to have emerged from the Caribbean."

Marley wore dreadlocks that hung down to his knees, a denim top, and brown trousers. Carrying a guitar over his shoulders, he shouted to the audience Pan-African prophet, Marcus Garvey's famous words: "A people without knowledge of their past is no better than a tree without roots." The audience shouted back the words in animated unison.

Five Reggae priestesses danced alongside Marley, swaying their arms from side to side, wearing woollen caps of the orange, yellow and green national colours of Jamaica, and long blue and brown dresses. The backdrop now featured a huge portrait of Ethiopian Emperor Haile Selassie, "the Lion of Judah," whom Marley and his followers had considered to be God's representative on earth. Selassie was, however, condemned to Limbo upon arrival in After Africa due to his human rights abuses, tyrannical rule, and for his godly delusions.

Marley broke into a rousing reggae number.

"What is he singing?" asked Cecil. "I can hear it's about Zimbabwe, but I can't understand his very strange accent!"

"It's a song," shouted Efua into his ear, "called 'Zimbabwe,' which was the former Southern Rhodesia. He wrote it to celebrate the country's independence in 1980!"

Cecil turned ashen, and squirmed as he stared

around at the predominantly black faces in the amphitheatre.

Marley belted one hit after another to the accompaniment of guitars and talking drums. He continued with "Africa Unite," calling on the continent to heed fellow Jamaican, Marcus Garvey's words to unite for the benefit of their people, urging them to move out of sinful Babylon and to their fatherland of Zion. The audience sang along the chorus, "We are the children of the Rastafarian. We are the children of the higher world."

As he performed, Marley skipped up and down the stage, his hand on his forehead, and his voice was so clear and melodious that it pierced the entire coliseum. The next song "Exodus" echoed the same message, leaving Babylon for a paradisiacal fatherland. During "Jammin," Marley pointed to the audience and sang, "I hope you like Jammin' too, Jammin' in the name of the Lord," as he stamped his feet and jumped up and down.

Turning his back to the audience, he then sprinted back and forth on the stage, and jumped up high as he chanted to the audience, "Roots, rocks, reggae." He staggered back to the microphone and roused the crowd to sing along to "Get up, stand up, stand up for your right, get up stand up, don't give up the fight." He then sang the lines that many After Africans considered heretical, "Most people think great God will come down from the sky, take away everything and make everyone feel high. But if you know what life is worth, you would look for yours on earth, and now you see the light, you stand up for your rights." After incredible renditions of "War," "Pimpers' Paradise," and "I Shot the Sheriff," Marley ended his set with the melancholy "Redemption Song," alone on stage playing a soulful guitar solo. As thunderous applause rang out, Efua told Cecil that both Marley and Fela had had huge funerals, and that after Marley's death, a massive storm had rocked Kingston, while rain and sunshine were simultaneously witnessed on the day of Fela's funeral in Lagos.

The South African singer Miriam Makeba emerged next, to loud chants of "Mama Africa" from the audience. She was wearing a costume made of leopard skin that had been given to her by the founding president of Kenya, Jomo Kenyatta, whose theft of large tracts of land in the Herebefore had landed him in Limbo upon arrival.

Makeba sported a short Afro, large round earrings, and intermittently flashed a beautiful smile. As the sounds of a bass guitar throbbed, her silky voice launched into the South African song "Mbube". The mammoth crowd started singing along, the coliseum shaking with the sweet rhythms. Makeba's performance veered from shy to sensitive to seductive as she explored the full range of her amazing voice.

"She wasn't only an international and Grammy-winning star during her life, she also energetically championed the anti-apartheid cause at the United Nations."

Cecil let this go without asking for an explanation. It was simply too loud here, and too difficult to hear.

Makeba then launched into the popular "Click Song," a wedding tune among her Xhosa ethnic group. Everyone in the coliseum roared as she clicked and danced her way through it. Next came the Brazilian song "Chove Chuva," accompanied by heavy percussions and Afro-Brazilian rhythms, in which Miriam asked God to stop the rain falling on divine love. Then came the poignant ballad and dark, haunting rhythm of "When I've passed on," which clearly struck a chord with the mighty throng of departed souls listening to her. She continued this sad mood with the melancholic melodies of "Sophiatown is Gone". As Makeba launched into the calypso rhythms of the Afro-Caribbean "Mighty Little Flea," she rolled her eyes, asking where this little flea had gone. Next was the sub-regional anthem "Mayibuye," in which Makeba pleaded for Southern Africans to come together to solve their problems, inspired by forefathers and kings such as Chaka, Lobengula, Moshoeshoe and Luthuli. She continued with the popular Swahili hit "Malaika" which got the After African throng off their feet.

Efua turned to a now enthralled Cecil as Makeba sang, explaining how one could hear the pain of an entire continent and its diaspora in her voice.

"This confirms the great African American writer Maya Angelou's idea," she said, "of why the caged bird sings".

Cecil grew nervous again as Makeba launched into her last song, "Kilimanjaro", a homage to Africa's highest mountain, located in Tanzania. One should "Kill the savage lion," she sang, "before the lion kills you".

A slender, pale-faced youthful-looking musician was next to emerge from the bottom of the stage amidst thick white smoke. He stood motionless for two minutes to soak up the adulation of the ecstatic audience.

"This is the African American superstar, Michael Jackson," explained Efua. "He was the iconic King of Pop, selling a staggering 750 million albums over four decades beyond the grave."

Jackson launched into "Wanna Be Startin' Something," displaying the full range of his meticulously choreographed moves. The performance included visuals projected onto a giant screen behind the singer. In "Thriller" and "The Way You Make Me Feel," he danced playfully behind beautiful, slender black models. In "Beat It," "Bad," "Smooth Criminal" and "You Rock My World," he played the tough gangster trying to make bad guys change their way through dance. In "Billie Jean" and "Remember the Time," he used magic to turn into a cat. The highlight of the show was an absolutely riveting performance of "Human Nature" in which Jackson contorted his body as if suffering massive electric shocks.

Cecil was dazzled by the unbelievable vocal talent and electrifying dance moves of the slight figure on stage. Jackson then broke into "I Will be There," a moving ballad in the Negro spiritual tradition, in which a higher being pledged to be there for Michael in his darkest hour of need, even as a glorious winged angel from the sixth heaven descended onto the stage to embrace Jackson, causing the already elated audience to ululate and roar out their approval. Then the angel took wing and left, leaving the crowd dazzled and awed.

"Earth Song" depicted a Garden of Eden being destroyed by human wars and offered a frightening image of nuclear Armageddon, with zebras, giraffes, and elephants all dying out, only to be revived by the Pied Piper of Pop's tuneful ballad. After a series of enthralling hits and amazing dance sequences, Jackson left the stadium in an astronaut's outfit, levitating over the audience to the booming announcement, "Michael Jackson has left the stadium."

A beautiful woman in a sequined dress then appeared on stage and began to sing in the most beautiful voice Cecil had ever heard.

"Who is that?" he asked Efua in wonder.

"Whitney Houston," came the reply. "She died tragically at the age of 48, a result of drug use, but was an extraordinary talent."

Whitney sang two of her ballads, "The Greatest Love of All," and "I Will Always Love you," as members of the massive audience joined hands and swayed from side to side, singing along. She was then joined on stage by three older women, who Efua explained were the legendary African American, multiple Grammy-winning soul songstresses, Ella Fitzgerald, Sarah Vaughan, and Aretha Franklin.

Yet another diva then stepped forward in an elegant multi-coloured sequined silk dress. Efua turned to Cecil, and whispered, "That is Umm Kulthum from Egypt. She was the greatest singer in North Africa and the Middle East. It was often said that the whole Arab world stood still each time she performed. The Egyptian leader Gamal Abdel Nasser who is here in the audience – used her patriotic songs and Pan-Arabism to maintain support at home and abroad, timing his key broadcasts around her concerts. She had learned to sing as a child by reciting Koranic verses dressed as a boy. It was also said that her voice was so powerful that it could shatter glass."

"I once dreamed of building a railway from the Cape to Cairo," replied Cecil. "Ran out of time, I'm afraid."

Umm Kulthum then launched into a medley of her melancholy operettas with her amazing voice dripping with *shaggan*, emotional yearning.

Next was Cheikha Remitti, as Efua explained, the woman dubbed as the grandmother of Algerian *rai* music, a form of blues. Remitti had cut her teeth singing with itinerant female musicians, known as *meddhahates*, before becoming one of the greatest *cheikhas*, the fabled women singers of western Algeria around the port city of Oran.

Remitti launched into her controversial, provocative song "Charrag Gatta," urging female virgins to "Tear, lacerate!" She sang her raunchy lyrics with great feeling and in a thick Arabic dialect. Backing up her raspy voice were the hypnotic rhythms of the *guellal* drums and the *gasba*, a desert flute. She teased the audience with her fluttering eyebrows, shimmying shoulders, and glistening eyes. She sang irreverently about the pleasures of alcohol ("Some people adore God, I adore beer"), the chauvinistic attitude of old men to younger brides ("Who would bring repugnant saliva together with sweet young saliva?"), and she closed with a song on the nostalgia of exile.

To end the Celestial Concert, a medley group assembled on stage to perform: Luther Vandross, Marvin Gaye, and Prince sang sultry ballads. A star-studded orchestra consisting of Duke Ellington, Louis Armstrong, Dizzy Gillespie, Charlie Parker, Ray Charles and Miles Davis (with his back turned to the audience) played some of the most melodious jazz After Africa had ever heard. The great James Brown together with the recently arrived Little Richard tore up the set with scintillating dance moves and funk tracks in their Afro and straight perms respectively, tottering platform shoes, and wide-sleeved shirts. And Tupac Shakur and The Notorious B.I.G. held hands in a historic reconciliation and frenzied celestial celebration of gangsta rap, which Cecil found difficult to regard as music at all.

The Fifth Heaven:
The Afrolympics

At the end of this enthralling Celestial Concert, Efua and Cecil left the giant amphitheatre. After ascending yet more hills, they arrived at a huge Olympic-size stadium shaped like a calabash. Scores of thousands of departed souls were still filing in for what appeared to be another spectacular event. They could see before them an orange tartan athletic track, a large square field, and a manicured soccer pitch in the middle of the floodlit stadium. As the athletes filed out in their glossy running outfits and colourful spikes, a huge cheer went up among the mammoth crowd.

"Welcome to the Afrolympics," said Efua. "This event in the fifth heaven showcases the athletic achievements of Africa through the ages."

"Afrolympics? Ah, you mean the African Olympics no doubt."

Efua nodded.

"So Frenchman Pierre de Coubertin's bright idea took off. I remember reading with excitement about the first Olympics in Athens in 1896. Actually, I was very keen on watching sport myself, though I was too sickly at the time to partake. Didn't exactly have the right physique. I even made sporting prowess one of the criteria for my own scholarships to Oxford University. I really believe leadership is fostered through sport, and that the 'heaven's breed' – sorry! No pun intended! – of young men who went abroad to run the British empire were fed a diet of sport at public schools like Eton, Harrow, Rugby, Dulwich, King's Canterbury, Tonbridge, Charterhouse, and St Pauls. So I'm looking forward to this. Let the games begin!"

Even as the first track event began, Efua kept up a tireless commentary for Cecil's benefit. Jesse Owens, the African American legend of the 1936 Olympic games in Berlin, repeated his success by winning the 100 and 200 metre sprints as well as the long jump. The crowd cheered thunderously, standing to catch a glimpse of the superstar's fluent, natural running style with its quick short stride, even as he accelerated away from his competitors.

Efua whispered to Cecil that Owens had embarrassed the German dictator, Adolf Hitler, by shattering his myth of a superior white Aryan race. "Hitler actually left the Olympic stadium in Berlin in disgust after Owens had won." Cecil looked totally confused, and had no idea whom these characters were.

The huge crowd then witnessed Uganda's John Akii-Bua tear up the track to win the 400 metre hurdles, as he had done at the 1972 Olympics in

Munich. Then came the women's track events, and a loud cheer went up as the flamboyant African American athlete, Florence Griffith-Joyner, stepped out in her space outfit and trademark extreme fingernails amidst a loud chorus of "Flo-Jo!" She easily won the 100 and 200 metre races, as she had done at the 1988 Olympics in Seoul. Griffith-Joyner arrived in After Africa before her time, dying young at the age of 38 of an epileptic seizure, having faced allegations of steroid use during her career.

The Afro-Brazilian triple-jumper, Adhemar Da Silva, then emerged to wild applause. He readied his thin frame and tall body before launching into a sprint down the track and executing the hop, skip, step, and jump with such elegance and strength that he sailed out to the gold medal as he had done at the 1952 Helsinki and 1956 Melbourne Olympic games. Kenya's Naftali Temu won a tactical 10 000 metre race as he had done at the 1968 Mexico Olympics, heralding a period of Kenyan dominance of middle- and long-distance running. Thunderous cheering erupted around the giant bowl as the bare-footed Ethiopian athlete, Abebe Bikila, entered the stadium to win the marathon event at the Afrolympics, as he had done at Rome in 1960 and Tokyo in 1964. Efua informed Cecil that Bikila was the first ever athlete to have performed this double feat.

As the athletics competition concluded, two teams of footballers in jerseys emblazoned with the map of Africa in the colours of the flags of Africa's 55 countries and matching socks, then walked onto the field as the crowd erupted into thunderous screaming. Efua whispered to Cecil that the teams were about to play for the Africa Cup of Liberation. She explained that an Algerian side – the Desert Foxes – would meet a Rest of Africa team. The Algerian team was made up of members of the group of European-based professionals who had abandoned their club sides in 1958 to tour the world for four years on behalf of Algeria's independence army, the National Liberation Front. Cecil now recalled what his Algerian ferryman had been telling him in the rocking canoe while crossing the River Africa.

"Ten of these players had been in the French national squad that was to play in the World Cup in Sweden that year," said Efua. "Their withdrawal was a major blow to the French team. The Algerian rebels played football to raise awareness of the brutal French imperial war between 1954 and 1962, which resulted in one million deaths, mostly Algerian. These players thus gave up fame and fortune for the greater cause of their country's liberation."

Cecil looked uncomfortable, and took a slow sip of Scotch, looking away again.

Up front with the pacy Eusébio spearheading the attack for the Rest of Africa was Nigeria's gangly striker, Rashidi Yekini, who, like Eusébio, had played in Portugal. Efua explained, "Yekini helped his country win the African Cup of Nations in 1994, where he was the top scorer and player of the tournament. He arrived in After Africa, having died early at the age of 48."

As the match got underway, The Rest of Africa's Afro-Brazilian Garrincha's mazy dribbles and close ball control dazzled the huge crowd. Algeria's lightning quick winger Said Brahimi – who had played professionally in France before the grave – scored two goals, while former French international Abdelaziz Ben Tifour captained the team brilliantly. The match was won by the Rest of Africa 3-2, with goals from Eusebio, Yekini, and Garrincha. After 90 enthralling, heart-stopping minutes of entertaining soccer, the players embraced each other, Eusébio received the Africa Cup of Liberation, and the crowd rose to its feet in unison to applaud the beautiful game.

As the audience roared their approval, the soccer stadium was converted into a tennis court. Onto the grass court stepped a tall African-American man with a prominent Afro.

"That is Arthur Ashe, who won the US and Australian Open tournaments, as well as Wimbledon, in a glittering career that saw him rise to the top of the world rankings. He arrived in After Africa early at the age of 49. The main stadium in Flushing Meadow, New York, where the US Open is played in the Herebefore is now named after him."

On the other side of the court, two women were hitting shots to Ashe across the net. Efua once again whispered to Cecil, "That is Alethea Gibson on the right. She was the first ever black person to win a tennis Grand Slam, and was crowned champion in the French Open, Wimbledon, and the US Open. She later competed as a professional golfer.

"On her left is Australia's Evonne Goolagong-Cawley. She won seven Grand Slam titles in Australia, the US, Wimbledon, and France. The best woman player in the world of her era, she was born of Aboriginal parents, black people against whom, as you know, the British committed a most heinous genocide. Between 1788 and 1901, colonialism reduced the indigenous population from 750 000 to 50 000, mostly through violence, dispossession, and diseases like smallpox." Cecil again turned red, and lit another cigarette.

Following three gruelling sets, Gibson and Goolagong-Cawley defeated Arthur Ashe by two sets to one, with the audience screaming their approval at every explosive serve, exquisite lob, and powerful dropshot.

A large screen above the giant stadium then switched from tennis to cricket. Members of the West Indian cricket team which went unbeaten in Test matches for 15 years, appeared, all clad in white, to roars of approval. The bespectacled, cerebral captain, Clive Lloyd, marshalled the team. Viv Richards coolly chewed gum as he smashed his way to multiple centuries. Michael Holding, Malcolm Marshall, and Joel Garner rained down bouncers on fearful opponents. Gary Sobers, the legendary West Indian all-rounder, was next on the screen to display his outstanding batting and bowling skills. The segment concluded with West Indies' Brian Lara batting his way to a dazzling world record of 375 runs.

As the cricket ended, a 7-foot 7-inch giant, South Sudanese US-based professional basketball player Manute Bol who had arrived in After Africa at the age of just 48, then walked to the centre of the stadium, accompanied by the recently arrived 41-year old African American, Kobe Bryant, to deafening applause. They pointed to the screen which paraded basketball stars from Africa and its diaspora: African Americans Wilt Chamberlain, Kareem Abdul-Jabbar, aka Dr J., Magic Johnson, Isiah Thomas, Michael Jordan, Allen "The Answer" Iversen, and Le Bron James, as well as Nigeria's Hakeem "the Dream" Olajuwon and Dikembe

Mutombo from the Congo, all performing acrobatic monster dunks to roars from the crowd.

The final event of the Afrolympics then flashed up on the screen. It was a replay of the famous 1974 Rumble in the Jungle. As more cheers rang out from the teeming audience, a dancing Muhammad Ali and snarling George Foreman stepped into the ring in Kinshasa, capital of Zaire, to fight for the boxing heavyweight championship of the world. Efua whispered to Cecil that this fight had been one of the greatest sporting events before the grave. "Foreman had never been defeated and had been expected to knock out Ali, the Louisiana Lip, who had converted to Islam. Ali was a great symbol of Black Power who fairly recently arrived in After Africa, and had chosen to go to jail in defence of his beliefs rather than fight America's imperial war in Vietnam. This had led to his suspension for three years. Ali was stripped of his world heavyweight boxing title. We all stayed up late in Ghana and across Africa and its diaspora to watch the fight on our black-and-white television sets.

"The muscle-bound, intimidating 24-year old Foreman was thought to be too much of a match for the 32-year old Ali. The Congolese crowd was, however, overwhelmingly on Ali's side."

On the massive screen Ali employed his famous

rope-a-dope tactic: covering his face, dancing around gracefully, and leaning on the ropes. He taunted Foreman to throw more punches saying, "They told me you could punch as hard as Joe Louis, George! Is that all you got, George?"

Though Ali was able to deflect many of Foreman's punches with his quick feet and skilful weaving and bobbing, he took some ferocious shots from Foreman. Ali also landed some hard jabs on his fearsome foe in the fourth and fifth rounds. He allowed Foreman to punch himself into a state of exhaustion and frustration, and then in the eighth round, Ali struck decisively. He danced away from the ropes and threw a series of hooks that staggered Foreman before a sharp left to the head and hard right to the face sent the champion tumbling to the canvass like a giant baobab tree. As Foreman lay dazed on the floor, the After Africa crowd roared in unison, "Ali! Ali! Ali! You are the Greatest." The multiple cameras in the stadium then zoomed in on a smiling Ali standing, bowing, waving and soaking up the adulation of the large crowd.

The giant screen went blank, signifying the end of the Afrolympics. Amidst much excitement, the throngs filtered out of the giant arena, chatting and recounting some of the amazing athletic feats they had just witnessed.

Cecil John Rhodes didn't share in the excitement. A complex feeling that was strangely familiar settled down on him. It took him a while to recognise it – the sense of disappointment in himself, of shame, that had so oppressed him as a sickly boy watching the others play rugby.

The Hotel Afropurgartorio

Following the exhausting journey through After Africa's five heavens, Efua explained to Cecil that it was now time to rest, as his two-day trial would begin the next morning in the fifth heaven. An anxious Cecil continued to ask about the trial, and Efua calmly assured him that all would be revealed by the next morning. They walked for about 20 minutes, and Cecil was shown into the Hotel Afropurgartorio which was more comfortable than luxurious.

Before she left, Efua noted that she was obliged, as his guide in the Hereafter, to inform Cecil about the sixth and seventh – and highest – heavens in After Africa. "The sixth heaven is where the angels reside, practising their celestial hymns and plotting strategies for saving souls in the Herebefore. Several of the performers you saw in the concert in the fourth heaven have become angels who regularly entertain the gods in the seventh heaven. As you saw, one of the angels was involved in Michael Jackson's performance during the Celestial Concert.

"The seventh heaven is the hallowed abode of Africa's gods, and is where After Africa's most eminent ancestors reside. The inhabitants of After Africa often recall that the Yoruba Supreme Being, Olodumare, formed a holy trinity similar to the Christian tradition: Olodumare Nzame, Baba Nkwa, and Olofi. Olodumare Nzame created heaven, the earth – with its animals and plants – and the moon, the sun, and the stars. This supreme deity then created man – whom he called Omo Oba – from mud, to rule over the earth. When Olodumare discovered that Omo Oba had become vain and arrogant, he instructed Nzalam, the lightning bolt, to destroy the earth. Omo Oba had, however, been created immortal and fled to the bowels of the earth where he took the name Olosi. He resurfaces periodically to incite mortals to break Olodumare's laws."

Efua paused to drink some water from the gourd around her waist.

"Olodumare then created a new mortal man to have dominion over the earth, named Obatala, thus beginning the lineage of the Orishas, or deities. Obatala had a son Aganju, the fire-breathing warrior God, and daughter Yemoja, the moon and water goddess. Aganju married his sister who gave birth to a son, Orungan. The child was so handsome that his father died of envy. On growing up, Orungan fell in love with his mother – what Europeans would refer to as the Oedipus complex – and committed incest with her. A grief-stricken Yemoja cursed her son, who died shortly after. The mother in turn climbed a high mountain in the ancestral Yoruba town of

Ile-Ife where she in turn died of heartbreak.

"Upon her death, her stomach burst open to give posthumous birth to a pantheon of a dozen Yoruba deities: Sango, god of thunder, fire, and lightning; Ogun, god of iron and war; Osun, goddess of the Osun river; Oya, goddess of the river Niger; Ifa, god of impossible things and palm trees; Osoosi, god of the hunters, birds, and wild animals; Oba, a river goddess; Orisa Oko, the hunter god; Obaluaye, god of illness and suffering; Dada, god of abundance; and Ibeji, the twin deities of fertility and rain-making. All reside in the seventh heaven of After Africa.

"The Nilotes – from South Sudan to northern Uganda to western Kenya – meanwhile believe in a force called Jok, which cannot be seen, but is omnipresent in the wind, air, trees, rocks, and hills. This deity is a life-force and can also be found in the seventh heaven."

Cecil began fidgeting, but Efua continued, "There is also a section of the seventh heaven inhabited by the Egyptian deities Osiris, Anubis, Heh, Atum, Thoth, and Maat. These gods still sometimes perform the 'weighing of the heart' ritual in the fifth heaven to determine how far new arrivals at this level can ascend. Yet another section of the seventh heaven bears a striking resemblance to the snow-capped Mount Kenya, which is where the ancient Kikuyu House of Mumbi believe that the first human being was created. They also believe that the mountain is an abode of the divinity. Next to that section dwells Kintu, the first human being on earth, based on the beliefs of Uganda's Buganda kingdom. Kintu descended from the sky with his wife Nnambi Nantuttululu who resides with him in the seventh heaven, as well as her brother Walumbe (Death)."

After providing this detailed orientation, Efua bade farewell to Cecil, promising to pick him up at the crack of dawn the next morning to escort him to his trial. He thanked his generous guide, biting down his anxiety, and waved her goodbye as she vanished into the dark night.

Back in his new quarters, Cecil took a long shower, admiring the bronze taps and amenities of the hotel, which seemed to have a strange sense of timelessness. He reflected on everything he had seen, returning to his astonishment at the remarkable achievements of Africa and its diaspora in the fields of history, culture, peacemaking, economics, literature, music, and sport. For him it was as unexpected as it was unimaginable.

II

The Counsel for Damnation

As the cock crowed to announce a new dawn, Efua arrived at the Hotel Afropurgatorio to pick up Cecil. He was waiting for her.

"Hope you slept well?" she asked.

"Yes, thank you", he said apprehensively.

They then walked together in total silence for about ten minutes before arriving at the calabash-shaped Olympic stadium where the Afrolympics had taken place the day before. Loud, thunderous rumblings were emanating from the massive crowd.

"I take it I'm to be fed to the lions," Cecil said, not quite succeeding in hiding his anxiety.

"Well, this is a trial that all souls have to undergo in After Africa. The process will shortly be revealed to you. I must admit though that there is going to be far more interest in yours than most."

He had to be content with that.

The stadium erupted in large roars as the crowd spotted Rhodes. Many stood up from their seats to get a better glimpse of the arch-imperialist. Efua took a visibly apprehensive Cecil to a large chair at the front of the stage, which was shaped like a huge court room, and gestured to him to sit.

"Good luck, Mr Rhodes. I will come back to escort you to your hotel at the end of proceedings today, and then bring you back for Judgment Day tomorrow."

"Thank you," he said quietly.

He felt totally alone. Looking around the vast throng of what seemed to him at least a billion departed souls, he recognised many of the people he had seen in his journey through After Africa's five heavens. But the crowd was bigger than those he had witnessed during the Celestial Concert and the Afrolympics, increasing his sense of trepidation.

The mass of departed African souls that had gathered to witness the trial of Cecil John Rhodes was indeed titanic. As the huge crowd grew even larger, seven eminent judges took up their seats on large golden thrones at the back of the stage, all appearing by virtue of some celestial thaumaturgy to be giants compared to Cecil and those in the audience. This seven member Council of the Wise who would judge this case consisted of eminent individuals from each of Africa's five sub-regions and two from its diaspora distributed through the US, the Caribbean and South America.

The Nigerian jurist Taslim Olawale Elias was the Council chair. He was introduced to the crowd by fellow member of the Council of the Wise, Wangari Maathai.

"Fellow After Africans, our eminent chair, Judge Elias was the first African President of the International Court of Justice – the World Court – in The Hague, where he served concurrently on the Permanent Court of Arbitration. He helped to draft the Charter of the Organisation of African Unity in 1963 and chaired the legal body that created its Mediation, Conciliation, and Arbitration Committee. Judge Elias also served as Attorney-General and then Chief Justice of Nigeria's Supreme Court, before being head-hunted to serve on the World Court for 15 years until he arrived in After Africa. He believed strongly in the contributions of every civilization, including African ones, to creating universal norms of international law. His legal scholarship thus sought to correct some of the Eurocentric misrepresentations of Africa. Elias was a man of tremendous erudition who published about 20 books and scores of articles on international law. He was renowned for his impeccable integrity before the grave."

Soaking up the warm applause from the crowd, Elias sat looking regal in the finely embroidered traditional robes common among his Yoruba people of southwest Nigeria. To his right sat the woman that had just introduced him, the Kenyan environmental campaigner, Wangari Maathai whom Rhodes had encountered in the second heaven among the Guild of Nobel Laureates. She represented Eastern Africa and was clad in a colourful East African dress of the green, black, and red colours of the Kenyan flag, with matching headgear. To Elias's left was Patrice Lumumba, an anti-imperialist fighter and the martyred first prime minister of the Congo. He represented Central Africa, and wore a white toga with a heavy gold chain, and his unmistakable large round-rimmed glasses. Next to him was Egypt's Boutros Boutros-Ghali, Africa's first United Nations Secretary-General. He represented North Africa. Dressed in a smart grey suit, cream shirt, and red tie, he looked the consummate diplomat that he had been in the Herebefore. Beside him on the extreme left flank was martyred South African scholar-activist, Ruth First, representing Southern Africa, dressed in a designer bright yellow African outfit, golden ear-rings, and her trademark black Gucci shoes. Next to Maathai on the right sat Maya Angelou who represented the African diaspora. She looked graceful in a smart black dress and matching shoes, with her grey hair and ready smile making two dimples in her cheeks. At the extreme right flank was Toussaint l'Ouverture, hero of the nineteenth century Haitian revolution, in a light-brown double-breasted suit with a waistcoat and a red and blue tie in the colours of his country's national flag, complete with its coat of arms. He represented the Caribbean and South American diasporas.

Judge Elias then rose from his large throne and walked purposefully to the large podium in the centre of the stage, where he opened the massive black Book of Life. Amidst loud applause, he called for calm, and began to speak.

"We are all gathered here in After Africa for the trial of Cecil John Rhodes."

Elias glanced down at the Book of Life.

"Cecil Rhodes was born in the English town of Bishop's Stortford on 5 July 1853 where his father, Francis, had been the vicar of the Hertfordshire town and his mother, Louisa, a housewife. Rhodes came to South Africa at the age of seventeen more to improve his health than his wealth, hoping that the dry African air would cure his weak lungs. He started by working on his brother Herbert's cotton farm in Natal. Rhodes, however, soon left to seek his fortune in the diamond fields of Kimberly. He quickly enjoyed spectacular success, establishing monopoly control over 90 per cent of the world's diamonds and much of its gold, having formed De Beers Consolidated Mines in 1888 at the age of only 35. Rhodes subsequently obtained a royal charter to set up the British South Africa Company, which effectively occupied and settled whites in what we rightly call Zimbabwe today.

"Mr Rhodes was an expansionist empire builder. Zambia and Zimbabwe were originally named after him, respectively Northern and Southern Rhodesia. One of his lieutenants ran what was known as Nyasaland, now Malawi, and he ensured British 'protection' for Botswana and Lesotho. He nearly took central Mozambique from the Portuguese, as well as Zaire's copper-rich Katanga province from the Belgians.

"Rhodes's 'empire' consisted of nearly 100 ethnic groups speaking 75 languages. He served as prime minister of Cape Colony. At the apogee of his power, he was toppled by the Jameson Raid in which his trusted lieutenant, Leander Starr Jameson, sought to overthrow Paul Kruger's mineral-rich Boer Republic in the Transvaal, in order to gain control of its gold mines. Rhodes's premiership ended in disgrace when he was forced to resign after the ill-fated attack. This incident put paid to his enduring dream of uniting the white 'races' of South Africa.

Ironically, it helped sow the seeds of the Anglo-Boer war, with all its bitter consequences. Rhodes's reputation never fully recovered from this debacle. His health deteriorated, and he died in his cottage in Cape Town's Muizenberg in 1902, at the age of 48."

Elias turned to Rhodes: "You have been in Limbo for 120 years. You have been shown the glory and achievements of Africa in your journey through After Africa's five heavens. You will now be tried in this fifth heaven for five crimes committed in the Herebefore. First, mass murder; second, racism; third, grand theft of Africa's natural resources and land; fourth, exploitation and enslavement of African workers; and fifth, egotism and a vainglorious quest for immortality."

The mammoth crowd stirred and started to chat animatedly among themselves, deeming these to be among the most serious charges they had ever heard in a trial in After Africa.

Judge Elias quietened the audience again, and continued, "It is therefore European imperialism as a whole that is on trial over the next two days, and you are the greatest individual symbol and embodiment of this phenomenon in the Victorian age. This is therefore the trial of a system, and not just of a man."

Elias then put the heavy Book of Life down,

and the two Counsel for Damnation appeared and took seats on the left of the massive stage. They were South African writer, Olive Schreiner, and Zimbabwean historian, Stanlake Samkange.

A huge ovation then rose from the crowd, as the two Counsel for Salvation appeared and walked to the right hand side of the stage. A thunderous crescendo of noise built up, and the crowd now screamed in unison, "Madiba!" "Madiba!"

Nelson Mandela, former South African president and Nobel laureate, had arrived. He was dressed in the traditional Xhosa outfit: a kaross he had worn in one of his trials by the apartheid government in the Herebefore. He pumped his fist in the air to acknowledge the lively After African crowd.

Beside Mandela was Harry Oppenheimer, the South African mining magnate, who had chaired Anglo-American corporation, part of De Beers Consolidated that Rhodes had established. Both men took up their seats on the right side of the stage.

Ruth First then rose slowly from her grand throne and addressed the crowd.

"Good morning, After Africans. It is my great pleasure and honour to read the citation for Olive Schreiner, who was also one of Africa's most famous novelists. Her book *The Story of An African Farm*, written at the age of 28 and set in the Karoo, has remained a classic in the Herebefore. Born of missionary parents and growing up on an African farm, Schreiner became a governess. The central character in her book, Lyndall, was a strong, unconventional woman whose rebellious search for social freedom within the constraints of her age led to marginalisation and loneliness: similar to the experiences that Olive herself suffered. Her feminist tract, *Woman and Labour,* was a seminal document in the struggle for the emancipation of women, critiquing the oppression of women and the limitations of their entering some of the same fields of employment as men."

First paused for effect.

"Here, I have to make a confession: I wrote a biography of Schreiner focusing on her pioneering role as a feminist. Olive had identified the predatory nature of capitalism and was particularly critical of mining capitalism. As she famously remarked. 'I'm always with the underdog, not with the top dog.'

"Olive was incredibly shy and plagued by personal insecurities. She had had no formal schooling, and endured long periods of non-productivity exacerbated by illness and self-doubt. She effectively defied her own class and race to stand up for her personal convictions; she suffered ostracism by many white South Africans as a result. Her willingness to uphold the courage of her conviction inspired my own activism and scholarship. Amandla!"

First pumped her right fist into the clear blue After African sky, as wild applause rang out across the huge arena that glistened in the glorious morning sun.

Elias then asked Schreiner – biting her nails nervously – to take the floor, after quietening the crowd. The writer gathered herself, and launched into her damnation of Rhodes in a posh English accent.

"Council of the Wise, and After Africans, I salute you all and recognise the huge responsibility that the gods of After Africa have bestowed on us today. I must first start with a confession: having met Mr Rhodes in the Herebefore, I often visited his opulent Groote Schuur estate in Cape Town and was good friends with the defendant, greatly admiring his boundless energy. Yet he was a shy, moody, secretive, narcissistic, impatient, ruthless, vindictive, and quick-tempered man. Within two years, I discovered that all the things I had heard about him being a benevolent philanthropist were a lie. I fell out badly with him, not because of unrequited love – as many scurrilously alleged – but because I was truly shocked by his unscrupulous business dealings, and his barbarous, cruel, and duplicitous imperial methods.

"Rhodes was a vain and dangerous egomaniac.

The 'Colossus' – as his mostly male friends who surrounded and fawned over him fondly styled him – in fact wreaked colossal devastation on Africa, and clearly suffered from delusions of grandeur. I thus unilaterally ended our friendship.

"It had been a strange, ephemeral liaison in which I was simultaneously attracted to and repulsed by Cecil. The straw that broke the camel's back for me was the notorious Strop Bill, which he pushed through the Cape Parliament when he was prime minister of the Cape colony. The bill allowed rural magistrates to order the flogging of what white masters regarded as disobedient black farm labourers. I described this draconian piece of legislation at the time for what it was: 'Every Man Wallop His Own Nigger Bill.'

"Rhodes's support for a Cape minister accused of corruption also led to a rupture in our personal relationship. After his political downfall following the ill-conceived Jameson Raid in 1895, I expressed relief that the terrible power which had threatened to crush the entire Southern African sub-region had finally been broken. Cecil Rhodes embodied oppression, injustice, and moral degradation. That was his real nature."

Amidst wild applause, Schreiner continued, "I am particularly honoured to be here today to contribute to the damnation of a fellow English-descended South African. Based on my personal knowledge of Mr Rhodes, I will make the case for the two charges relating to mass murder and grand theft of Africa's mineral resources, and leave my fellow Counsel for Damnation, Stanlake Samkange, to provide more details of these, as well as of the other three charges relating to racism, exploitation and enslavement of workers, as well as egotism and a quest for immortality.

"First, it is important to note that one must unequivocally reject the argument of Rhodes's many apologists that he was a 'man of his times.' My parents were Christian missionaries who inculcated timeless values in me. Though Rhodes's father, Francis, had been the vicar of Bishop's Stortford, as we heard from Judge Elias, his son seemed, in stark contrast, to have abandoned the values he had been taught as a child. Even as Rhodes claimed to be doing God's work through his imperialism, this was clearly a case of God and the Devil marching in lockstep. The role of Christian missionaries in supporting Mr Rhodes's brutal exploits must be one of the most shameful episodes in the history of the Anglican Church. Many of Rhodes's contemporaries criticised him. I published *Trooper Peter Halket of Mashonaland* as a biting satire and critique of the brutal methods that he used to suppress the 1896 Ndebele and Shona uprisings after the theft and occupation by Britain of Matabeleland and Mashonaland.

"The book deals with Peter Halket, a young British soldier in Rhodes's British South Africa Company in Mashonaland, also known as the British Chartered Company. Halket employed the same racist and savage techniques and had the same avaricious appetites as his fellow conquistadors, until he got lost one night and met a Christlike figure who convinced him to change his ways. He freed a black prisoner, who was subsequently murdered, and Halket's own commanding officer then shot the young trooper dead."

As a hush fell over the crowd, Schreiner continued. "Her Majesty's government – though the British are often erroneously credited with a sense of fair play – had granted Rhodes a royal charter, by means of the company I have just named, to annex territory north of the Limpopo. Mr Rhodes was allowed to do this, if necessary by dispossessing the indigenous inhabitants and offering British mercenaries land ownership in exchange for military conquest. This was 'Perfidious Albion' at its most hypocritical, treacherous, and rapacious. British people simply turned a blind eye to the savage slaughter, accompanied by widespread rape, whipping, and lynching of black populations. They chose instead – like the proverbial ostrich – to bury their heads in the sand and to focus on the 'glory' of empire. I therefore felt it important to open British eyes to the cruelty being perpetrated in their name, and my novel on the fictional Peter Halket was one of the earliest attempts to do that. By 1890, Mashonaland had been seized, while whites staked out farming claims in Matabeleland six years later. In my book, I unequivocally condemned Rhodes and his murderous mercenaries in the British South Africa Company who pillaged, enslaved, and stole the land of the Shona in Zimbabwe, even as they greedily pursued mineral wealth."

Schreiner paused to drink a glass of water before continuing. "The Ndebele and Shona were treated by Rhodes's troops with unbelievable cruelty and contempt, and their grievances at the mass murder of their people, theft of their land, and rape of their women eventually led to renewed rebellion. Rhodes negotiated a treacherous and dishonest accord in which the Ndebele and Shona were allowed to return to their land over which all rights had been revoked. He then employed military means to subdue the Shona, using the political support of Whitehall and the economic resources of the British Chartered Company.

"Rhodes had hoped to find great mineral wealth in the conquered land he immodestly named 'Rhodesia,' just as he had been the most successful beneficiary of the gold and diamond rushes in South Africa in the 1870s and 1880s. As I noted before the grave, this period was the saddest in the history of any Anglo-Saxon people. I think Rhodes realised he did not have long to live, and took short cuts, often acting impulsively in many of his duplicitous dealings. He drank like a fish, consuming champagne, stout, whisky, and a Russian liquor called kummel. I have no doubt that this contributed to his suspect judgment, mood swings, impulsive behaviour, and *folie de grandeur*.

"I often told my friends at the time that Rhodes was like Peter Pan: a little child who had never quite grown up. History and geography were his favourite subjects as an adolescent student. He used to like playing soldiers as a child, using his younger siblings as troops. As an adult, he often compared himself to a Roman emperor. These were the imperial delusions he clearly sought to fulfil in adulthood. However, many of his adult ideas were puerile and immature. He was never known to have had intimate relations with any women, appeared to me to be asexual, and surrounded himself with male acolytes who all worshipped him. Rhodes was morally dangerous. As I once wrote to my brother about Rhodes's methods, 'A man may wriggle and wriggle and wriggle, and creep safe out of everything, and with his skin whole' – but at the cost 'of everything that makes life worth living, namely honour, manhood, courage!' That is the man who stands accused before you."

The crowd rose to their feet and gave Schreiner a rousing standing ovation, as she walked off the giant stage, bowing to each member of the Council of the Wise. She looked at Rhodes disdainfully as she walked past him.

Judge Elias turned to Rhodes, who had been scribbling frantically with his left hand as Schreiner spoke, and asked whether he wanted to respond to any of her arguments. Having been listening intently, Cecil leaned forward and rubbed his florid face, and replied shrilly, "Yes, please, Your Honour. I must say that I find it grossly unfair that a fellow English-born South African and former good friend would do such perfidious injury to my character. Olive referred to me in the Herebefore as 'the only big man we have here,' meaning in Africa. Four years after she ended our friendship, she still referred to my 'gifts of insight and genius'. Even when she was upset with me, she wrote a short satirical sketch in which she condemned me as a heartless capitalist, but noted that my 'great stature' would prevent me from being condemned to hell. With nowhere else to go, my character was allowed to enter heaven, her fictional angels noted that 'With God all things are possible.' Even though I was not religious in the Herebefore despite my church upbringing, I trust that Olive's satire will be acted on in After Africa following this trial. I should add that her book on Peter Halket was dismissed by many critics as an embittered political pamphlet full of 'absurdity and hysterical passion,' and I could not agree more."

Rhodes then threw his head back and put his hand in his tweed jacket pocket. He smiled.

"Despite Olive's criticisms, she admitted even after we had fallen out that she admired my genius while detesting my methods. She confessed that she respected my strength, while sympathising with my weaknesses. She dedicated her Peter Halket novel to Sir George Grey, a former British Governor of the Cape Colony whom she described as a 'great good man' of 'incorruptible justice and a broad humanity, representing the noblest attributes of imperial rule.' But like me, Grey was a political pragmatist. He had come to the Cape from New Zealand, having subdued the Maoris through the same divide and rule tactics that I used in Southern Africa. After all, these were tried and tested British imperial methods. The Maoris, in fact, described Grey as 'crooked as a snake.' He then employed the very same tactics to pacify the Cape, seeking to co-opt the Xhosa into colonial society by making them labourers in the cash economy. It is thus not fair of her to dedicate that book on my alleged exploitation to a man who employed similar tactics that were not only acceptable in our day, but were honoured!"

Virulent booing and hissing spread through the crowd.

Elias again quietened the stadium, before Patrice Lumumba strode across the stage, to wild cries of "Patrice! Patrice!' in order to deliver a short citation introducing Stanlake Samkange.

"Fellow After Africans. Some of you are aware that the esteemed Zimbabwean Professor, Stanlake Samkange, was one of the most prominent historians in the Herebefore, with his 1978 *Origins of Rhodesia,* having won the prestigious annual Herskovits prize of America's African Studies Association for the best book on Africa. Having returned to his country after independence from teaching in America, he drove around Harare in a Rolls Royce and lived in a castle-like fortress. Samkange arrived in After Africa at the age of 66. I can think of no person better qualified to conduct the damnation of Cecil Rhodes than he. Thank you for your kind attention, and you will hear more from me tomorrow on Judgment Day."

Lumumba strode back elegantly to take his seat on the golden throne to more loud cheering. Elias then invited Samkange to deliver his damnation.

Dressed in a dapper grey suit with a smart waistcoat, a bright yellow tie, and a white handkerchief in his pocket, the second Counsel for Damnation stepped forward to deliver his own testimony. Placing his pipe, which he had been smoking, carefully on the lectern, Stanlake began:

"Your Honour, I don't really want to get embroiled in this English civil war between Olive and Mr Rhodes! My purpose here is to provide – as meticulously as an erudite historian with an academic scalpel can – evidence for the damnation of Rhodes, one of the most odious of imperialists whom I had had his father try in the latter's church in Bishop's Stortford in my 1967 novel *On Trial for My Country*.

"I would first like to expose Rhodes's grand theft of African land and resources as well as the mass murder that he perpetrated against an estimated 60 000 Africans. He had the support of the British government, which awarded his British South Africa Company a royal charter in 1889, which significantly was four years after the notorious Conference of Berlin. This conference effectively set the rules for an orderly partition of Africa so that the European powers could amicably divide our continent up between them as if they owned it. Now what was this royal charter that the British South Africa Company received? It was a formal grant enabling them to seize, administer, and populate our land with white settlers. As Adolf Hitler did four decades later in relation to Germany and Europe at large, Rhodes argued that he needed to settle surplus British populations on African lands. He proceeded to dispossess black people of their ancestral lands in what is now Zimbabwe and Zambia through aggressive and duplicitous means, stealing three and a half million square miles of black territory in one of the most ignominious land-grabs in modern history. It was often said during the imperial era that trade followed the flag. Rhodes, in fact, inverted this saying, with the British government following his lead and lending political, economic, and military support to his mercenary and mercantilist adventures.

"Not being satisfied with having cornered diamond and gold production in South Africa and establishing global monopolies, Rhodes was determined to find another El Dorado flowing with gold in Matabeleland and Mashonaland. He used his agents to negotiate a concession with the Ndebele king, Lobengula, who naively believed that he had only ceded limited mining rights, but ended up losing his entire country to Rhodes. Mr Rhodes then arranged for one Grobler, a representative of the Boer Republic to Matabeleland, to be murdered, and instigated Reverend John Moffat, an assistant to the administrator of Botswana, to meet with the illiterate Lobengula in 1888. Moffat then claimed to have signed an agreement with the King to forbid the sale or lease of any part of his country, or enter into any treaty, without the approval of the British government. Lobengula denied this, having only agreed to peace and friendship between the Amandebele and the British.

"As I have consistently noted, Moffat's version was a huge, monstrous naked lie. Rhodes used this duplicitous 'treaty' to keep Germany, Portugal, and the Boers out of Zimbabwe. In the same year, he sent emissaries – led by Charles Dunnell Rudd, his business partner – to agree a deal whereby Lobengula would receive one hundred British pounds a month, one thousand rifles, and one hundred thousand cartridges, in exchange for a grant of mineral rights in Matabeleland and Mashonaland, and the exclusion of all other parties from the territory.

"Jameson then started recruiting mercenaries for the Pioneer Column in 1890 in search of their African El Dorado. Each man was offered a 6 000-acre farm and fifteen underground and five alluvial gold claims if found on land that they would steal. The British South Africa Company gave itself the right to half of the loot, with the rest being shared out among the assorted motley crew of settlers, freebooters, mercenaries, and adventurers.

The huge herds of Ndebele cattle would also be divided between these armed thugs and the British South Africa Company. Rhodes drew up a secret contract promising two rough freebooters – Frank Johnson and Maurice Heany – a total of £150 000 and 110 000 acres of land to command the white mercenaries to destroy Lobengula's rule. The British government further provided imperial troops, with the prime minister, Salisbury, preferring to conquer other people's land as cheaply as possible. As the German chancellor Otto von Bismarck had famously remarked, 'The Englishman is like the dog in the fable. . . . The dog who cannot bear that another dog should have a few bones, although the overfed brute is sitting below a bowl full to the brim.' Even as the British government professed its peaceful intentions to Lobengula, Jameson continued plans for a conflict which was launched without any ultimatum or declaration of war, despite the legal fiction of earlier treaties having been agreed with Lobengula, such as the Moffat Treaty and the Rudd Concession. Jameson also lied to British representatives that Ndebele warriors were endangering white settlers in the territory. Rhodes himself lied that the servants of white settlers were being slaughtered by Ndebele fighters. Emissaries whom Lobengula sent to the British were taken prisoner and shot dead."

"Rhodes's methods often relied on subterfuge and dishonesty. They were shockingly brutal. This Charter Law, or 'Charter Ro' as it was called, was used to kill indigenous Mashona through a psychopathic Rhodesian police chief Captain Lendy, who was later promoted to magistrate. A letter by Queen Victoria to Lobengula was replaced with a forged one by Rhodes and Jameson, containing very different terms. In two incidents in 1892, at least thirty locals were summarily executed after a Frenchman was murdered and a white Rhodesian had his goods stolen. Rhodes also ordered that expenditure in the country that his company was running be reduced from £250 000 a year to £36 000, while the police force was reduced from 700 to forty. This was 'imperialism on a shoestring.' It was backed by an understanding that Rhodes could count on British funding and troops to subsidise his grandiose ambitions in a murderous quest for gold and to subdue the 'rowdy natives.'

"Rhodes and his associates cynically manufactured a *casus belli* to wage a war that destroyed Matabele power between 1890 and 1893. He used scaremongering tactics with the British government, warning that Germany, Portugal, or the Boer Republics would grab power in Zimbabwe if he did not do so on behalf of his native country.

Using the false premise that the wire of the British South Africa Company had been stolen, Rhodes's men seized all African cattle in the surrounding area, many of them belonging to King Lobengula. This was clearly a provocative scorched earth policy that could only lead to starvation. Led by his trusted lieutenant, the racist Leander Jameson, they then killed thirty of King Lobengula's men. Jameson and Lendy blatantly lied that the Ndebele had killed 400 men, women, and children in a bid to recover their cattle, while in fact seven fatalities had been reported by eyewitnesses. Other lies were spread about Lobengula's fighters, that they had destroyed crops, looted homesteads on white farms, and killed farm workers.

Samkange paused to relight his pipe, puffing until thick clouds of tobacco smoke hung over him on the giant stage.

"By 1893, in order to steal the land of Matabeleland and the gold that was believed to be underneath it, thousands of fighters of the cornered King Lobengula were massacred by Rhodes's 900-strong mercenaries. The maxim gun was particularly prominent in these one-sided battles. Captured black prisoners of war were summarily executed against all legal conventions. Kraals were burnt, and thousands more innocent people were massacred. Farms were carved out of stolen land in choice, well-watered locations, and prospecting claims were laid over Matabeleland. Thousands of Ndebele cattle were stolen by Rhodes's men and driven into pens in Bulawayo.

"And the devastating consequences of this military aggression and conquest? Tens of thousands of Ndebele men, women, and children were starved to death due to the theft of their cattle. Many were prevented from ploughing their lands and sowing seed until their surrender could be proved to their conquerors. Their crops were burned, thus preventing them from sustaining their livelihoods. The charges of mass murder against Rhodes are therefore irrefutable. This was a catastrophic war of aggression waged against a defenceless Ndebele nation."

Samkange looked down at his written notes and continued, "Lobengula, before he died in flight and was secretly buried, belatedly recognised in a telegraph to Rhodes, 'I thought you had come to dig for gold, but it seems you have come not only to dig for gold but to rob me of my people and country as well.' The Zimbabwean King would later describe white men as 'fathers of liars.' As Olive Schreiner noted earlier, Rhodes's brutal rule led to another uprising by the Ndebele in 1896 which was also brutally suppressed. The share of their stolen land and cattle that was promised to them was not returned, and indigenous populations were moved by their white conquerors to badly watered land unsuitable for farming.

"Rhodes's imperial greed to conquer and possess territory was insatiable. He patronisingly stated that 'Africa is the last uncivilised portion of the empire… and…it must be civilised.' Given his destructive legacy of empire-building, Mr Rhodes must be condemned for his imperial crimes.

"He was petrified after the disgrace of the Jameson Raid in 1895 that the names of both Rhodesias would be changed, and asked apprehensively, 'Did you ever hear of a country's name being changed?' His worst fears were eventually realised. Northern Rhodesia became Zambia, and the statue of Rhodes in Lusaka was toppled when they achieved independence in 1964. Southern Rhodesia became independent Zimbabwe, and after 1980 they wiped clean the streets of Harare and Bulawayo of his statues. Both countries sought to remove the imperial stain by rebaptizing themselves. South Africa has only belatedly started a debate on the numerous Rhodes memorials that still litter its post-apartheid landscape. As we heard from the Herbefore, students at the University of Cape Town toppled a statue of Rhodes prominently displayed on its campus in 2015, at a time when its main hall, the very centre of its graduations and other ceremonies, was still named after Rhodes's racist and destructive lieutenant, Jameson. Rhodes University in Grahamstown had earlier quietly removed a bust of the man after whom it was named from its main entrance to avoid a debate about renaming the university."

The After Africa masses started discussing these shocking details animatedly among themselves, before Elias again asked for silence.

Samkange continued, "As for the charge of racism, Rhodes is clearly guilty as charged, and there is incontrovertible evidence of his prejudice in many of his utterances, as documented in my 1982 booklet, *What Rhodes Really Said about Africans*. Since many of these racist attitudes have persisted in the Herebefore, I really wonder whether there is something in the British psyche that makes racism and prejudice so widespread. The self-inflicted wound called Brexit, whereby Britain left the European Union after a referendum, was, after all, largely a nativist anti-immigrant vote. Even before apartheid was passed into law in 1948, as prime minister of the Cape Colony between 1890 and 1895, Rhodes was its forerunner, helping to curtail black voting rights through introducing new property and educational criteria. Rhodes told the Cape parliament in 1887, 'The native is to be treated as a child and denied the franchise. . . . We must adopt a system of despotism, such as works so well in India, in our relations with the barbarians of South Africa.'

He also once reprimanded a police officer in Matabeleland in 1897 for having spared the lives of Ndebele rebels who had pleaded for clemency, saying, '…you should not spare them. You should kill all you can, as it serves a lesson to them… They count up the killed, and say so-and-so is dead and so-and-so is no longer here, and they begin to fear you.' Rhodes's credo of white supremacist thinking can, in fact, be summarised by his statement, 'Treat the natives as a subject people as long as they continue in a state of barbarism and communal tenure; be the lords over them, and let them be a subject race and keep the liquor from them.'"

The audience gasped, and many had begun weeping at these unbelievably offensive utterances. Rhodes had turned a dark red, and reached for the whisky flask which he fumbled nervously to remove from the pocket of his tweed jacket, and furtively sipped from it.

Elias again asked for calm and Samkange continued.

"Rhodes is also guilty of the charge of exploitation and the enslavement of black workers. He practised a half-baked social Darwinism in which the fittest were to survive and the weakest –

like the dinosaur and the dodo – would become extinct. Working with Afrikaner legislators in the Cape parliament, as prime minister, Rhodes restricted the size of African-owned freeholds and inheritance rights, and forcibly removed blacks to native reserves through the 1894 Glen Grey Act – a precursor of apartheid's notorious Bantustan policies by half a century. Rhodes further pushed the Cape parliament to introduce hut and labour taxes on blacks in order to force them into the cash economy; packed over 11 000 black miners into inhumane, dog-patrolled, wire-protected barracks; and supported draconian labour laws like the 'strop bill' that Olive Schreiner referred to earlier, in order to facilitate the continued supply of human fodder to his mines while impoverishing the black population. Rhodes effectively sought to build the British empire on the backs of cheap black labour, virtually slave labour. As premier of the Cape Colony, he also introduced social segregation – later to be called apartheid – for indigenous people in schools, hospitals, prisons, sport, and public transport; forced blacks to carry passes – a precursor of the apartheid 'dompas' – and removed thousands of members of these groups from the colony's electoral rolls. It is thus crucial to demythologise the cult of Rhodes that has been so carefully cultivated by legions of his fanatical supporters since his death in 1902."

Samkange took a few more puffs on his pipe, but it had died again. He put it back on the lectern, and continued, "Rhodes is also guilty of egotism and a grandiloquent quest for immortality. His scholarship scheme at Oxford University, which started after his arrival in After Africa in 1902, sought to create a breed of largely Anglo-American 'rulers of the world' from the British Commonwealth and Germany. Over 6 000 scholars – most of them overwhelmingly white American, Australian, and Canadian males from outside Africa, from where this wealth was stolen – studied at Oxford within a century of Rhodes's death. He perceived the English as 'God's chosen instrument in carrying out the divine idea over the whole planet.' He proclaimed that 'the more of the world we inhabit, the better it is for the human race'. Rhodes insisted on being buried in a granite rock in the sacred Matopos hills of Zimbabwe, predetermining the inscription on his grave, and looking down on people in a country he had conquered for eight decades, until Zimbabwe won its independence in 1980. His burial place became a Valhalla, a shrine and place of pilgrimage for Rhodesians and South Africans, including assorted racist white supremacists, imperialists, and members of the British royal family.

"Rhodes confirmed Vladimir Lenin's belief that imperialism was the highest form of capitalism, harnessing political power, as prime minister of Cape Colony, as well as economic power, as a diamond and gold magnate. He used his economic wealth to buy political power, and employed political power to protect and extend his wealth. He perverted politics as he had business, using patronage – in the form of shares or land – to buy off politicians, as he had bought out diamond prospectors, in Britain and South Africa. This included members of the Afrikaner Bond with whom he established an alliance in the Cape parliament in order to pass harsh legislation against blacks and to protect white Afrikaner farmers.

"Rhodes was thus a ruthless and unscrupulous businessman and politician. He was a monopolist both in terms of territorial expansion and control of diamonds and gold. In cornering the diamond industry in Kimberley, he ruthlessly crushed many smaller businesses, and defrauded many of his opponents. He manipulated the stock exchange and bought off people with company shares, outright bribes, and job offers. It has been indisputably proved that he had speculative shares in a shell diamond company in the early 1880s. He bought off rival entrepreneurs, politicians, and journalists to further his expansionist goals. His character was often autocratic, brutal, and bullying. Many saw him as a ruthless megalomaniac, even in his day. In order to secure a royal charter, he misled investors and the British government into believing that his British South Africa Company owned the Rudd Concession. He continued to control the company even after he was compelled to surrender his directorship after the Jameson Raid.

"As we learned from beyond the grave, South African historian, Bernard Magubane, who is here with us in the audience, condemned Rhodes as 'a robber and a racist to the core who ruthlessly, cynically pursued his goals. No shortcut was too dishonourable for him to use to achieve his vision. He was possessed of imperial greed and insatiable rapaciousness.' British South African Paul Maylam, a historian in the land of the living, wrote an epitaph to Rhodes's unscrupulous greed which was equally devastating: 'In reflecting on the life and career of Rhodes I find little to redeem him. I have not come across a sentence spoken or written by him that is inspiring or uplifting; his utterances range from the ordinary to the abhorrent. His crude racist outbursts have been well documented. He possessed an authoritarian personality, and some of his ideas about empire were puerile. His methods were often dubious or despicable... Rhodes does not deserve to be rehabilitated.'"

Elias again turned to the imperialist in the dock and asked whether he had anything to say in his defence against these very serious charges.

Rhodes got up slowly. His face was pale, he was sweating profusely, and his hands trembled.

"My lord, I cannot deny that these incidents took place. However in my defence, these were the moral standards of the age. Otto von Bismarck, to whom Professor Samkange referred, once noted that making laws is like manufacturing sausages; it is better to see the end product than the messy process itself. One has to break a few eggs to make an omelette. So also was imperialism. It was a system in which the end justified the means, and this was a civilising mission on behalf of primitive barbarians that I felt at the time would continue living in trees and caves."

The crowd objected loudly to this racist language. Judge Elias quietened the audience, and turned to Rhodes, "I hope you are aware of how serious the charges levelled against you are. Criminal charges of this wide-ranging kind in After Africa are very rare. I would really advise you to choose your words very carefully."

"I am sorry, Your Honour," replied Rhodes. "Even though my father was a vicar in England, as has often been mentioned, I never went to church and considered Table Mountain – that's in Cape Town –

as my chapel where I could experience spiritual moments. The religious teachings I learned as a child included not merely devotion to God, but to Queen and country as well. I believe that through my imperial exploits which augmented the British empire in Africa, I did fulfil these teachings. Queen Victoria was, after all, head of the Church of England, and British missionaries were key allies of imperial expansion, constantly urging onwards our Christian soldiers, encouraging us to convert and civilize the heathen African 'sons of Ham.' I must note, in my defence, that I took Lobengula's sons into my own home after he had ceded his kingdom to me. Is that evidence of racism?

"Let me tell you that my main aim was to unite Southern Africa in a customs union. In fact, and most genuinely, I was the *first* contemporary Pan-Africanist."

The crowd burst into wild laughter. Rhodes's face darkened, either in defiance or shame, or perhaps both. He lit another cigarette as Judge Elias again calmed the teeming throng.

Elias then ceded the floor to a gesturing Stanlake Samkange to respond to the defendant.

"I must just quickly respond to Mr Rhodes's exaggerated claim that he looked after Lobengula's sons. These children were treated not as adopted sons but were humiliated as servants. It was widely reported that when one of the sons asked to visit 'Rhodesia' with Rhodes, the imperialist told the boy, 'Now if you come up with me, I must have no nonsense about your being a king. You will have to wash plates and clean my boots.'

"On another occasion, in front of assembled guests, Rhodes callously asked Lobengula's sons as they worked in his garden at his lavish Groote Schuur estate, 'Let me see, what year was it I killed your father?' and then laughed loudly. These are scarcely examples of caring for the children of the vanquished king.

"My fellow Counsel for Damnation, Olive Schreiner, lived in the same era and was subject to the same empire and exposed to the same colonial values. Yet she categorically rejected the despicable imperial values that Mr Rhodes embodied and sought to defend here, attempting as he does to justify the unjustifiable. Even in Rhodes's own day, many people in England and Southern Africa condemned his awful methods. There were, after all, abolitionists who condemned slavery even when its practice was widespread. Rhodes's justifications of imperialism are therefore unacceptable and fly in the face of all the moral codes that we uphold here in After Africa. He has never been held to account for any of his heinous crimes, and nor has the system of Imperialism ever been tried and unequivocally condemned to eternal damnation. That is why Rhodes – as the greatest embodiment of the imperial age – must surely face damnation in hellfire for all of eternity."

The crowd rose to their feet and gave Samkange a standing ovation for his eloquent and meticulously detailed testimony. Cecil lit another cigarette, and continued to sweat profusely. Olive Schreiner ceded her right to a closing statement, and the audience waited with bated breath for the defence of the two Counsel for Salvation.

III

The Counsel for Salvation

Rhodes sat motionless in the middle of the stage in a much smaller chair beneath the seven giant golden thrones of the Council of the Wise. His confidence was somewhat lifted as he looked across at the Counsel for Salvation – Nelson Mandela and Harry Oppenheimer – two high profile figures who were about to defend him. Mandela and Oppenheimer sat directly opposite the stage from the two Counsel for Damnation – Olive Schreiner and Stanlake Samkange – who remained on the stage on the left side to observe the rest of the proceedings.

Judge Elias welcomed both men warmly. Maya Angelou then rose to deliver the citation for Mandela, to ringing applause.

"Greetings fellow After African citizens. Based

on the warmth of the reception, this man clearly needs no introduction. Nelson Rolihlahla Mandela was one of the greatest moral figures of the twentieth century. He spent 27 years in jail before going on to become the first democratically elected president of South Africa. Winner of the Nobel Peace Prize in 1993, he was a nation builder par excellence who did the most to unite a South Africa divided for decades by colonialism and apartheid, and on the brink of a potential civil war. Madiba – as he was fondly called by his clan name – embodied a prophetic leadership style that eventually freed his people from the bondage of apartheid. During his five year presidency, he sought to reconcile his society, heal a conflict-ridden continent, and build bridges with the African diaspora. His leadership thus represented prophetic nation building, continental renewal, and diasporic solidarity. The charisma of this founding father helped South Africa's young, democratic institutions to flower, and gave the country an international stature of which the former global pariah could never have dreamed. Mandela's stature in his lifetime was comparable to that of George Washington and Mahatma Gandhi."

As the crowd burst into applause, Maya gestured to them for calm. Turning to Judge Elias, she noted, "If I may Judge Elias, I would just like to read a brief extract from my poem to Mandela on the announcement of his demise and impending arrival in After Africa:

> *Your man of strength, Gideon, emerging*
> *triumphant...*
> *we watched as the hope of Africa sprang through*
> *the prison's doors.*
> *His stupendous heart intact, his gargantuan will*
> *hale and hearty...*
> *No sun outlasts its sunset, but it will rise again*
> *and bring the dawn.*
> *Yes, Mandela's day is done, yet we, his inheritors,*
> *will open the gates wider for*
> *Reconciliation....*

As Angelou walked back to her seat with applause ringing in her ears, Mandela stepped forward stiffly amidst yet more thunderous applause. The former South African president walked slowly but purposefully to the lectern amidst a standing ovation. He bowed in acknowledgment at the applause, adjusted his kaross, and gestured for silence, before taking off his glasses and starting his defence in his slow, purposeful voice.

"Thank you, your honour, for this early opportunity to test out our legal skills in our first trial in After Africa. We enjoyed very much our role as a defence counsel in the Herebefore, and hope that we can do a good job here today. Many people in the audience must be surprised that a liberation fighter like myself could have been selected by the gods of After Africa to defend this arch-imperialist, Cecil Rhodes, seated here before us. First, I should note that there are some similarities between Rhodes and I: both of us were among the most well-known historical figures in African history; we both had countless books, documentaries and monuments devoted to us beyond the grave; both of us have had universities and streets named after us; we were both Anglophiles – and I famously got on well with Queen Elizabeth II – though Mr Rhodes was, of course, born in England before moving to South Africa; we both trained as lawyers, and pursued our degrees part time; we were both awarded honorary doctorates by the University of Oxford; and both of us spent much of our lives in Cape Town, with Mr Rhodes living in the opulence of the Groote Schuur, his grand estate at the foot of Table Mountain, which became my official residence in Cape Town as president. Before that, of course, I had lived in jail in Cape Town, mostly on Robben Island, for a third of my life.

"The five charges for which Mr Rhodes is being tried here today – mass murder, racism, grand theft of African resources and land, exploitation and enslavement of African workers, and egotism and a quest for immortality – are very serious indeed. I will not attempt to deny these charges, as that would be difficult to do historically and empirically. What I would want to do instead is to plead for clemency on the basis of the defendant's other great achievements. Even though Cecil Rhodes and his associates exploited the resources of Southern Africa and enriched themselves at the expense and exclusion of the black masses, they were undoubtedly pioneers of the world-class mining sector that still remains the backbone of the South African economy. I will focus particularly on Mr Rhodes's contributions to the field of education, and allow my fellow Counsel for Salvation, Harry Oppenheimer, to set out Mr Rhodes's achievements in the areas of economic development and entrepreneurship. We hope that these great feats will help assuage the justifiable anger of the revered gods and ancestral inhabitants of After Africa at some of the more sordid aspects of an individual I myself referred to in the Herebefore as a 'robber baron who enriched himself at the expense of others'."

Rhodes turned bright red in his chair, and lit another cigarette as he peered nervously into the increasingly restive crowd.

"I personally took the decision in 2002," continued Mandela, "to link my name permanently to that of Mr Rhodes when we established the Mandela Rhodes Foundation during the centenary celebrations of the great imperialist's death. The Rhodes Trust had contributed ten million pounds for the foundation to provide scholarships for African students to study in South African universities, provide children with better healthcare, and to tackle poverty, illiteracy, preventable illnesses, and homelessness. This Foundation continues to contribute enormously to the development of South Africa and Africa before the grave.

"We launched the Mandela Rhodes Foundation in the magnificent Westminster Hall in London in 2003, with the then British prime minister, Tony Blair, and former US President and former Rhodes scholar, Bill Clinton, in attendance. Mr Rhodes was clearly the dominant figure in colonial society by the end of the nineteenth century, while the last decade of the twentieth century saw the achievement of democracy and the end of apartheid, marking one of the last colonial experiences in Africa. I argued, during the launch of our foundation, that the bringing together of the names of Rhodes and Mandela represented a symbolic moment in the closing of a circle with the larger historic circle, and a coming together of two strands in our history.

"I strongly believed that we had to harness all the diverse strands of our history to reconstruct and develop our new country. We had to promote both continuity and change, and to ensure that all South Africans were convinced that the nation belonged equally to all who lived in it. I felt that this symbolic act would demonstrate the country and its citizens coming together across historical divides to build a new society.

"Mr Rhodes's former company, De Beers, under the Oppenheimers, demonstrated their commitment to transformation and reparations by donating the magnificent Rhodes Building in downtown Cape Town – originally commissioned by Mr Rhodes himself – to the Mandela Rhodes Foundation. The Oppenheimer's Brenthurst Foundation further supported black economic empowerment in post-apartheid South Africa. Mr Rhodes would have been proud of these efforts to make the South African economy fit for purpose in the twenty-first century. The Mandela Rhodes Foundation has undoubtedly improved the lives of South Africans and Africans, supporting over 500 scholars from 28 African countries to study in South African universities. Mr Rhodes was also a great entrepreneur who left most of his wealth to support scholars from across the world who have benefitted from his scholarships for well over a century.

Mandela paused and gazed around at the crowd, as if to gauge their reaction.

"In the second century after Mr Rhodes's death, it was an appropriate sign of global responsibility that the Rhodes Trust decided to redirect some of these resources back to Southern Africa, where the wealth had been generated in the first place. I am sure that Mr Rhodes would himself have identified with this wise decision to establish a foundation to build human capacity in contemporary South Africa, allowing the country to remain a globally competitive economy as it had been in the diamond and gold-mining sectors in which he operated during his era. Even though the name Mandela was being yoked to that of Rhodes, 'Mandela' represented, in a real sense, every single South African and African: the farmers who labour to produce bountiful harvests on African farms; the girl child fighting for an equal opportunity to receive a decent education; the neglected AIDS orphans; and the rural poor –whom our Martinican intellectual Frantz Fanon, here with us in the stadium today, famously described as 'the wretched of the earth' – who struggle to eke out a decent existence. It is on behalf of these marginalised groups – the voiceless and the powerless – that we decided to lend our name to this initiative. I am sure Mr Rhodes and I would have made common cause in this venture, and he is here to confirm this."

Rhodes nodded nervously in the middle of the

stage, as he lit another cigarette.

Mandela paused to drink some water, then continued.

"The British warden of the Rhodes Trust at the time, John Rowett, conceived and strongly pushed the idea of a Rhodes Mandela Foundation. I must however note that he controversially left his post as warden shortly after he had tried to move the Rhodes House library next to the toilets in the basement of the building in order to make room for a common room for Rhodes scholars! But Mr Rowett was a very nice man nonetheless.

"Though several people raised legitimate concerns about the decision to link our name to that of Cecil Rhodes, this initiative also had several extremely credible supporters who reassured us that we were indeed doing the right thing. Thabo Mbeki, my former deputy president, but by then the president of South Africa, was widely regarded as a major intellectual proponent of contemporary Pan-Africanism. He supported the creation of this foundation. Mbeki said, 'To place the names of Mandela and Rhodes side by side in this manner is an innovative, unusual, and visionary thing to do... Those aspects of Cecil Rhodes's otherwise contested legacy which can be put to work for the good of Africa, are being harnessed – in particular his legacy of excellence in education, and entrepreneurship...

While Rhodes's continental vision opened up Africa to Europe, Mandela's vision restores Africa to itself.'

Njabulo Ndebele, the erudite former vice-chancellor of the University of Cape Town and a trustee of the Mandela Rhodes Foundation, also noted at the time, 'Is it not remarkable that Rhodes's dream of inter-ethnic co-operation should, at this time in world history, combine with Mandela's dream of reconciliation, the latter encompassing a much more complex human environment?'" The large After African throng started to murmur, with many asking loudly whether this was really the same Mandela who had been such a great African liberator beyond the grave, as Elias again waved his arms in calling for calm.

A visibly rattled Mandela adjusted his kaross again, cleared his throat, and continued: "Mr Rhodes's contributions to education in South Africa are unparalleled. Rhodes University in Grahamstown in my native Eastern Cape is named after him, while the University of Cape Town was founded on land bequeathed to the university on a section of his Groote Schuur estate. Cecil Rhodes had always wanted to build a university on the foothills of Table Mountain and had started plans for it during his lifetime. UCT was thus a fulfilment of his inspirational dream. Rhodes University College was opened two years after Rhodes's arrival in After Africa's Limbo, with the Rhodes Trust and De Beers providing much of the funding. I myself studied in neighbouring Fort Hare, and remember Rhodes University warmly as a place that maintained cordial and dignified relations with my alma mater and its students. We often visited Rhodes University and were always treated with dignity and honour in a South Africa which at the time was seething with racism and inequality. We were particularly pleased to have received an honorary doctorate from Rhodes University. A marble bust of Mr Rhodes was placed at the main entrance of the university. The university's first women's residence, Oriel House, was named after Mr Rhodes's college at Oxford, although ironically the Oxford college was one of the last to admit women students!

"Rhodes University regularly commemorated Founder's Day on 12 September, the day of the founding of Southern Rhodesia. A Rhodes Commemoration Lecture was launched in 1970, with the first lecture delivered by my fellow Counsel for Salvation and friend Mr Oppenheimer. The fact that an effort to change the name of Rhodes University, which we privately opposed, was defeated in the university Senate clearly demonstrated the continuing clout and resonance of Mr Rhodes in post-apartheid South Africa. His name has thus become more closely associated with academic excellence than with exploitative imperialism. Interestingly, one of the names proposed as alternatives to Rhodes University during these fierce debates was 'Rhodes and Mandela University.'"

The After Africa crowd again became audibly restless, expressing amazement at what they felt was Mandela's disingenuous defence of Rhodes, before Elias again stepped in to restore order.

An increasingly uncomfortable Mandela wiped sweat from his brow with a white handkerchief.

"Further afield, Mr Rhodes has left more of a legacy at Oxford University in England – one of the world's most reputable institutions of higher learning – than any other individual. As earlier noted, he was awarded an honorary doctorate in Law by Oxford. Rhodes left £100 000 for his college Oriel in his will with which a new college building was erected and named after him. There are portraits of Rhodes in his college, as well as a Rhodes Fellow of Modern History at Oriel, and at an annual dinner, a toast continued to be drunk at the college to this generous benefactor. The Rhodes Scholarship is Mr Rhodes's most enduring legacy. He used a large part of his £3.3 million fortune to fund this scheme.

"Rhodes House in Oxford, which runs the scholarships, is one of the finest buildings in the city. It combines the warmth of Cotswold stone with classical architecture, African features – the

Great Zimbabwe soapstone bird towers over the building, while a circular slab from the Matopos Hills stands at the domed entrance hall – and it is crowned by a magnificent copper-domed rotunda. The building houses one of the finest libraries in the world regarding matters of the British empire and America, which serves both the university community and scholars who visit from across the globe."

Madiba took a final sip of water before concluding.

"Many people would know that I used to read the poem *Invictus* written by the English poet, William Ernest Henley, to strengthen my resolve while I was imprisoned on Robben Island. I want to repeat it here for emphasis:

> *It matters not how strait the gate,*
> *How charged with punishment the scroll.*
> *I am the master of my fate:*
> *I am the captain of my soul.*

"I would also finally like to end my plea for the Salvation of Cecil Rhodes by reading to you the eloquent ode by Rudyard Kipling, the great British poet and champion of imperialism, as an elegy to his friend, after Rhodes's death. It is called 'The Burial':

The immense and brooding Spirit still
Shall quicken and control.
Living he was the land and dead,
His soul shall be her soul!
It is his will that he look forth
Across the world he won—
The granite of the ancient North—
Great spaces washed with sun.
There shall he patient take his seat.
(As when the Death he dared),
And there await a people's feet
In the paths that he prepared.

There was loud booing, widespread hissing, tepid applause, and much confusion among the After African audience, as Mandela finished his defence. There was much disbelief and consternation at this defence of the arch-imperialist, and some called for Madiba himself to be tried for linking his name to that of Cecil John Rhodes. As Mandela returned to his seat, he politely shook hands with a beaming Cecil Rhodes as he passed by him.

Judge Elias again calmed the crowd, as Egyptian scholar-diplomat, Boutros Boutros-Ghali, stood up slowly from his golden throne and walked towards the middle of the large stage to read the next citation.

"Good afternoon, fellow citizens of After Africa. Harry Oppenheimer, like Mandela, was a nonagenarian when he arrived in After Africa. Like Rhodes, Oppenheimer was one of the richest men in the Herebefore. He was chair of Rhodes's De Beers Consolidated Mines for three decades, and chair of the Anglo American Corporation for a quarter of a century. Like Rhodes, he was at one stage also a politician, serving as a member of parliament for Kimberley. He financed the white so-called liberal Progressive Federal Party under apartheid, but his critics accused him of having exploited and underpaid his black workers."

The crowd again grew restless, and Elias had to stop the loud whistling.

The Judge then beckoned Oppenheimer to come to the lectern to deliver his defence. The mining magnate moved deliberately and confidently to fulfil his task, giving Rhodes a warm embrace in the middle of the stage as he passed him, before settling himself at the lectern.

"First, let me note what an honour it is for me," he began, "to have been invited to be a Counsel for Salvation to Cecil Rhodes, a fellow mining magnate and entrepreneur, and one of the most important historical figures in Southern Africa. I am, in a true sense, one of his heirs, having taken over the running of De Beers, a company he painstakingly built up through his intelligence and industry to become the world's largest diamond conglomerate. Rhodes's legacy is represented by countless biographies, novels, plays, monuments, memorials, universities, films, and documentaries in the Herebefore. This was a truly great man. I am glad that Mr Mandela has set out Mr Rhodes's great contributions to the cause of education in Africa. I myself supported the African National Congress financially at Mr Mandela's request. This cooperation continued under my son, Nicky, with Mr Mandela meeting regularly with businesspeople at our spacious Brenthurst estate after being released from jail, as well as after becoming president of post-apartheid South Africa. I also later learned that my company, De Beers, had provided funding for the Mandela Rhodes scholarship scheme.

"In defending Cecil Rhodes from what I consider to be rather unfair charges, I will stick closely to the text of the lecture I delivered at Rhodes University in 1970 to commemorate the centenary of Cecil's arrival in South Africa to which Mr Mandela referred earlier. In this lecture, I sought to reassess Rhodes's legacy and his relevance to Africa's contemporary problems at that time. I was born in Kimberley where Rhodes had made his fortune from diamonds, and as a child, I revered him as a hero. As an adult, I had worked in an environment shaped by Rhodes's ideas and personality. He was truly, in a genuine sense, a builder of modern South

Africa, as well as the father of modern Zimbabwe and Zambia. The story of Southern Africa cannot be written without considering the genius of this great historical figure. I know that Cecil's reputation took a hammering, as imperialism itself became discredited after African states gained their independence from the 1950s onwards. I also acknowledge that some of the methods he employed involved harshness and perhaps even deceit, but he certainly does not deserve to be judged so harshly in the Hereafter. Even if Cecil's methods could not always be condoned, they could be excused by the breath of his vision and his ultimate achievements, which doubtless benefitted the greater good. He never sought personal enrichment or power for its own sake, but used wealth and influence to secure a greater noble vision for mankind."

The After Africa audience again became agitated at what they considered to be the beatification of an unrepentant racist. Elias pleaded for calm, waving his hands frantically.

Oppenheimer had to raise his voice to continue, and only then did the crowd calm down.

"We must always remember that Rhodes was a man of his times, and a product of the Victorian age. His faults tend to be retrospectively and unfairly magnified, while his achievements are belittled and even discounted. Men of European descent in Africa were often illogically judged according to different and more contemporary standards, and I hope we don't adopt the same unfair measures in After Africa. We have to recognise that values are dynamic, and that they change over time, as society itself changes. So, while the use of force to pursue imperial aims was acceptable in Rhodes's days in civilised societies – particularly when dealing with tribal people – such methods were no longer acceptable by the 1960s."

The mammoth crowd in After Africa started protesting loudly at Oppenheimer's offensive speech, and Judge Elias admonished him, as he had earlier done to Rhodes, to watch the use of his language.

"Apologies, Your Honour, I did not realise that this phraseology could cause offence. I grew up in colonial and apartheid South Africa speaking like this without really experiencing any adverse reactions. Please, permit me to continue my defence. Cecil had great force of character, ability, and generosity, and devoted his entire 48 years on earth to doggedly pursuing his single-minded vision of a united Southern African confederation. He envisioned a space in which English and Dutch-speaking whites would unite South Africa, Northern and Southern Rhodesia, and Bechuanaland and Basutoland under the British flag, by means of rail, road, and telegraph. It is a gross distortion of the truth to claim that he was pursuing an illusory vision with means that were morally reprehensible.

"Rhodes may have conquered the Ndebele, but King Lobengula's kingdom simply had to be set aside because he was an obstacle to the imperial vision of building a modern federation in Southern Africa. Cecil has been unfairly and widely maligned for his conquest of Matabeleland, but he had respect and affection for the Ndebele, and did all in his power to advance their welfare to the extent possible. Rhodes was also the only man who demonstrated the courage and patience to make peace with the Ndebele. That is why they honoured him at his funeral in the Matopos Hills, giving him the royal salute that had never before been given to any white man.

"Cecil John Rhodes was deeply committed to human rights. He called for equal rights for all civilised men, even if that meant mostly white men who were literate and had property. Far from being just a crude imperial expansionist, he was the only man to have called for the elimination of the 'imperial factor' in Southern Africa. Though Rhodes spoke of Africans as children and barbarians and felt that they were centuries away from reaching equality with Europeans, as noted by Counsel for Damnation, Stanlake Samkange, he felt that this was mainly true of the mass of backward Africans, and that a few individual black Africans could become civilized as full citizens of his envisaged modern, industrial Southern African federation.

"Cecil, however, believed that the majority of Africans would need to continue to live a tribal life and contrary to his critics, the Glen Grey Act – which Olive Schreiner condemned earlier – was designed not to prevent Africans living and working outside their tribal areas, but to make fair provision for Africans who could not, or would not, live outside a tribal society. Rhodes also sought, through the provision of the so-called hut tax to find work elsewhere for those who could not find land on the reservations. He felt that he had to induce blacks to undertake manual labour and inculcate in them good Christian values emanating from the dignity of labour. He never thought that blacks could leave their tribal settlements to live in or near large urban areas. African reserves were thus not a retrogressive step but a protective and educative measure for backward people. Cecil would surely have expected these reserves to disappear as the need for them waned."

Judge Elias again cautioned Oppenheimer on his derogatory language.

Oppenheimer apologised gravely once more, and continued.

"Though Rhodes established a political alliance

as prime minister with the Cape Dutch, he realised that Paul Kruger's Transvaal Republic could never be part of his vision of a modern, industrialised Southern African federation, since it was too insular, self-satisfied, and indifferent to luxury. The Calvinist traditions of the Dutch would retard the Protestant capitalist work ethic that Rhodes was seeking to promote. Though the Jameson Raid which destroyed Cecil's political career and damaged his reputation may have been reckless and arrogant, one can understand it in the context of Rhodes's declining health, which made him impatient, as Olive Schreiner herself acknowledged. Knowing he might die soon, Cecil wanted to see his life's work fulfilled during his own lifetime: a totally understandable feeling for such a great visionary. I therefore do not believe in this much-repeated Shakespearean saying: 'the evil that men do lives after them, the good is oft interred with the bones.' I would rather associate myself with Rhodes's own saying: 'the work survives the worker.' Cecil's work remained unfinished, but still has much relevance in Africa beyond the grave."

"Rhodes's great vision was a major work of civilisation that was both regional and global. He dreamed of world peace and prosperity, guaranteed by irresistible Anglo-American power, harnessed to the industrial might of imperial Germany. Though he talked of the 'special quality of Nordic people,' I categorically reject the charges that these ideas were forerunners of German chancellor Adolf Hitler's racist Aryan ideas. Hitler hated Jews and exterminated six million of them. In stark contrast, a Jewish businessman, Alfred Beit, was Rhodes's friend and business partner, and he also admired his great rival, Barney Barnato, who was also Jewish and with whom he later formed De Beers Consolidated Mines. Though many critics retrospectively dismissed Cecil's ideas as anachronistic and impractical, I believe that the idea of superpowers guaranteeing world peace was one that continued to be the most realistic option for global peace, as demonstrated by America and Russia in my own lifetime. I mentioned that in Southern Africa, Rhodes sought to establish a federation under the British flag. The fact that Africans in the Herebefore formed organisations like the Southern African Development Community eight centuries after Cecil's death, involving all of these countries, shows what a great visionary of regional integration and development he was, and how his ideas retained much relevance. Rhodes was sentimentally a British imperialist, but also pragmatically recognised that his federation could only prosper under the protection of the British flag. This was a man ahead of his times who should be praised, not punished, for opening up Africa to Western infrastructure and industry as Mr Mandela noted."

Oppenheimer took a drink from a glass of water on the lectern, as the crowd grew increasingly restive.

"Perhaps Rhodes, the son of a vicar, recalled the biblical saying: 'And he stretched forth his hand to his disciples and said: Behold my mother and my brethren. For whosoever shall do the will of my Father which is in heaven, the same is my brother and sister and mother.' Rhodes was certainly a man who equated his desires with duty, and his plans with the provisions of God's providence. He really did believe that he was doing God's work. Cecil was clearly a colossus and a 'big man.' People either loved him or loathed him, but no one could ignore him. He was a charismatic man who could convince business associates and politicians to do what they otherwise might not have wanted to do. Just as he was no ordinary British imperialist, Rhodes was also no ordinary business tycoon. His iconic speech to the annual general meeting of De Beers, two years before his arrival in After Africa, is worth citing in this regard. In response to shareholders who questioned the wisdom and profitability of De Beers financially supporting the British South Africa Company to colonise Rhodesia, he made the distinction between unimaginative shareholders who spent their lives filling bags of money and then having their fortune squandered by their heirs on wine, women, and horses, and in stark contrast, imaginative shareholders who thought more long term, and recognised the strategic importance of European civilization North of the Limpopo. I often wish I had had the courage to address my shareholders in De Beers in such terms, but I never did!

"Rhodes used profits from diamonds to build railways across Southern Africa. He established a fruit farming industry in South Africa. He began the manufacture of explosives and fertilizers. He contributed greatly to developing gold mining in the Transvaal, and he funded the colonisation of Rhodesia. His use of diamond profits to develop the broader South African economy is a lesson that has continued to this very day in the Herebefore. These are no mean feats for one man in a single lifetime. Cecil wanted to build modern industrialised states in Southern Africa, and thus had to express his dreams in terms of profit and trade in order to have potential shareholders in his Chartered Company buy into his admittedly crude motto, 'Patriotism plus five percent.' But he uniquely recognised that political power needed a sound economic base to succeed. The juggernaut of economic development clearly destroys much that is useful and more that is beautiful, but in Rhodes's eyes, this was the price of the manifest destiny of mankind and the master plan of Almighty God."

Noticing that the large throng had become increasingly boisterous, Oppenheimer began his conclusion.

"Having myself studied at Oxford like Cecil Rhodes, I appreciated the foresight he showed in setting up the Rhodes scholarships, even though I unfortunately did not have the privilege to become one myself! Mr Mandela has made the case for the great success and impact of these scholarships competently, so I will not dwell on them. But I wanted to note in closing that the scholarships represent a distinguished brotherhood. Rhodes sought to provide his scholars with a liberal English education, based on the special comradeship and friendship of the city of 'dreaming spires' and 'home of lost causes' which I myself experienced at Christ Church college in Oxford. These scholars would, Rhodes hoped, develop a special outlook, and go out into the world to fulfil his grand visions. His ideas could then become not just actualised, but immortalized, through the actions of these brilliant men. Many people seek to preserve their memory through their family. Rhodes sought to preserve his own through his scholarships, and has succeeded spectacularly. Of that, there can be no doubt.

"In conclusion, I just want to say that I was

also privileged to have been the Chancellor of the University of Cape Town for over three decades, which, as has already been noted by my fellow Counsel for Salvation, Mr Mandela, was founded on Cecil Rhodes's Groote Schuur estate. Rhodes was a man of amazing historical vision and the builder of modern South Africa. That his visions and dreams are still alive and relevant in the Herebefore is the clearest sign of his greatness. He does not deserve to be punished for the five very serious crimes he is being accused of here. He should instead be praised for his contributions to regionalism, state-building, entrepreneurship, industrialisation, and education in Southern Africa. I end as I ended my Rhodes University lecture with the words of the Archbishop of Cape Town spoken at Rhodes's funeral sermon: 'Know ye not that there is a prince and a great man fallen this day in Israel.' I thank you for listening."

Amidst much booing and hissing, Oppenheimer returned to his seat next to Mandela, giving Cecil Rhodes another warm hug in the centre of the stage as he passed by him. Rhodes himself looked more relaxed than he had ever been during this trial, though he was still sweating and chain-smoking. He tried to take a swig of whisky too, but found that he had emptied his flask.

Judge Elias announced the end of the day's proceedings and asked that everyone return at dawn the next day. As the seven judges and four Counsel left the stage and the mammoth crowd started dispersing in animated discussion, Efua walked to the front of the stage to escort Rhodes back to the Hotel Afropurgatorio. They walked back in silence, and Efua bid him farewell, promising to arrive at the break of dawn to escort him back to face the delivery of his judgement.

IV

Judgment Day

Early the next morning, Efua again accompanied Cecil from the Hotel Afropurgartorio to the giant stadium where his trial was due to conclude. They again did not talk much as he arrived. She took him to the centre of the stage as the swelling crowd continued to gather for the *denouement* of this riveting trial. Smiling, Efua turned to Cecil and noted: "Farewell, and may the Council of Wise render its justice wisely."

Hands trembling, Cecil shook her hand and took out a cigarette. He lit up, and started smoking as he sauntered to his seat at the centre of the stage. On the left side of the giant stage sat the Counsel for Damnation: Stanlake Samkange and Olive Schreiner in animated conversation, while the Counsel for Salvation – Harry Oppenheimer and

Nelson Mandela – sat together in total silence on the right hand side of the stage.

Shortly after, the seven judges took up their seats on the large thrones on the huge stage. Judge Elias rose slowly to quieten the mammoth crowd. Reaching the podium, Elias cleared his throat, and set the massive brown Book of Judgment on a large lectern, and addressed the crowd.

"After Africans, I thank you for your great cooperation and civility over the last day of the trial of Cecil John Rhodes. I would like to ask that you extend to us this same comportment as we conclude this important trial by sunset today."

He drank some water, and continued. "Let me set out the rules of how we will arrive at a verdict in this historic trial. Firstly, having heard from the two Counsel for Damnation, as well as the two esteemed Counsel for Salvation, our seven judges – with five representing each African sub-region and two representing the diaspora – will take turns to announce their judgment. As you are aware, a unanimous verdict by all seven judges is needed to convict to the fullest sentence, while a majority will elicit a lighter sentence, and a minority will lead to the defendant proceeding to the sixth Heaven of After Africa. I will only intervene to cast my vote in the case of a tie among the six judges.

"Let me reiterate, as I did at the beginning of

this trial yesterday, that the imperialist Cecil John Rhodes is being tried here in this fifth heaven for five crimes committed in the Herebefore: first, mass murder; second, racism; third, grand theft of Africa's natural resources and land; fourth, exploitation and enslavement of African workers; and fifth, egotism and a vainglorious quest for immortality. We have heard from the two Counsel for Damnation and the two Counsel for Salvation. The seven judges in the Council of the Wise have also discussed the trial until the early hours of this morning. I now wish to invite each of them to deliver their individual verdicts."

Loud murmurings and animated discussions emanated from the crowd, and the air was thick with anticipation. Elias once more asked for calm. He then reintroduced the six other judges, inviting Boutros Boutros-Ghali to take the floor amidst raucous applause and shouts of "The Pharaoh! The Pharaoh!" As Boutros-Ghali strolled towards the giant podium, he cleared his throat and started to speak in a slow deliberate fashion, with his Arabic and French intonations coming through.

"Fellow After Africans. I am here to represent the sub-region of North Africa as a proud Coptic Christian Egyptian from the land of the pyramids in the Herebefore. In my previous life on earth, I was a student of International Law in the Sorbonne in

Paris, taught law at Cairo University for 28 years, was deputy foreign minister of Egypt for 14 years, and also served as the United Nations Secretary-General for five years where we successfully made peace in Mozambique and, outside Africa, in Cambodia, but also suffered huge failures in Rwanda, Angola, and Somalia. So, I believe I am eminently qualified to render this verdict. It is important to note, as African scholars like Kenya's Ali Mazrui who is here with us in the audience have done before me, that for several centuries, the rules of European statecraft legitimized the subjugation of non-Western societies. Millions of Africans, Caribbeans, Asians and South Americans thus fell under the sway of European 'sovereignty'. International law was therefore not only made by European nations, but was also substantially made for their self-serving imperial purposes. As has been consistently pointed out, this trial is not just about Cecil Rhodes as the greatest individual embodiment of nineteenth century imperialism, but it is also about the system of imperialism itself that is on trial with him."

The crowd burst into thunderous applause as Cecil nervously lit up another cigarette, and Elias called once again for calm.

"I once noted in the Herebefore that, I do not claim to elevate the vision of the *al-Madinah al-Fadilah* (The Virtuous City) called for by the medieval Muslim philosopher of the tenth century, Abu Nasr Al-Farabi to that of a Utopian world, for I cannot promise to go beyond what is feasible and what is possible.' I am thus not naïve about power politics, but I do feel that it is important to note the notorious European legal concept by which colonial territory was declared a no man's land – *terra nullius* in the legal jargon – on the spurious grounds that these territories were inhabited by 'native savages' in an era of a perverse Western *mission civilisatrice.* They could therefore be seized by, and carved out among, European colonial powers. It is this cultural arrogance that 40 African and Asian countries with populations of 800 million – over a quarter of the global population at the time – overturned in winning their independence during the famous Revolt against the West by 1960.

"We have already heard the overwhelming evidence against Cecil Rhodes presented cogently by Counsel of Damnation, Stanlake Samkange and Olive Schreiner, yesterday. I will thus not waste time going over these details again. I want simply to say that Rhodes is clearly guilty of mass murder, racism, and theft of land that clearly did not belong to him. All of these crimes have been criminalized under international law. I will leave the other charges for my fellow judges to comment on, but these are the three most relevant to my expertise and background.

I thank you all for listening."

Amidst loud applause, Boutros-Ghali adjusted his white *djallaba* and slowly walked back to take his seat on one of the seven golden thrones neatly lined up at the back of the massive stage.

Elias then summoned Wangari Matthai to take the floor, as the audience again burst into rapturous applause, amidst cries of "Earth Mother! Earth Mother." Resplendent in the same orange and black African dress with matching headgear that she had worn when she received the Nobel Peace prize in Oslo, Maathai began soberly.

"I am here as Eastern Africa's representative on the Council of the Wise in After Africa. I was born in the village of Ihithe in the background of the cloud-covered majesty of Mount Kenya. I drank water from the stream, but became conscious at an early age of the destruction of the country's forests by commercial plantations. As if by a prophetic vision from the ancestors of After Africa, at the age of 37, I began a campaign to save the country's forests and to fight for the plight of rural women. I eventually led the Green Belt Movement to plant 30 million trees across Africa. I also fought consistently for women's and human rights, successfully protesting the efforts of the corrupt and autocratic regime of Daniel arap Moi – who on his arrival in After Africa was banished to Africa's Hades following his trial – to build a high-rise office park in the green belt of Uhuru Park. I had defiantly noted then that, 'Our forefathers shed blood for our land.' I have also often repeated my credo that, 'We are called to assist the Earth to heal her wounds.'"

Maathai waited for the deafening applause to die down.

"I will focus today, based on my human rights and environmental backgrounds, on the following three charges: mass murder, racism, and theft of Africa's land. It is obvious as our Counsel for Damnation – the eminent historian, Stanlake Samkange – made clear yesterday, that Cecil Rhodes committed mass murder of black people on an industrial scale, and stole huge tracts of land in Southern Africa. These crimes are truly unforgiveable in the human and material cost that they wrought on the populations of South Africa, Zimbabwe, and Zambia. In my country Kenya, Rhodes's British compatriots also committed atrocities during the Mau Mau rebellion of the 1950s – including torturing, castrating, and raping Kenyans, and keeping them in concentration camps – for fighting for their freedom. That is why the system of imperialism of which Rhodes was the most famous proponent must not just be tried, but permanently criminalised. This should not be part of our values in either Africa or After Africa."

Maathai paused briefly to drink from a brown

gourd of palm wine.

"With regard to the third accusation, namely theft of African land, I wish to make a further comment based on my environmental activism. The racist Italian conquistador, Christopher Columbus – sponsored by the Spanish crown – transplanted flowers, plants, and animals from Europe to the Americas in the fifteenth century in a bid to recreate his homeland on another continent. This barbarous act destroyed indigenous plants and animals in the Americas. Rhodes committed similar environmental crimes in Africa. He introduced the grey squirrel into the South African landscape where it did not belong, and this rodent became a pest to the African environment. Rhodes similarly introduced llamas, deer, fallow, and kangaroos to the South African landscape, while Corsican pines displaced local fynbos. In trying to recreate his native England in Africa, Rhodes did not only steal our land, he degraded it. I think it is no exaggeration to say that he is also guilty of what I would describe as "ecological imperialism".

"However, let us be clear that this is a digression from our central task, which is to determine if the defendant is guilty *as charged*. On the basis of the impeccably presented, detailed evidence we have heard, I find the defendant guilty as charged of mass murder, racism, and theft of African land."

As Maathai moved to sit down on her throne, huge applause and whistling rang out across the giant coliseum. Cecil Rhodes sat stoically in his small chair at the centre of the stage, staring into the ground, seemingly hoping it would swallow him up. Drops of perspiration fell from his forehead, and his hands trembled as he reached for a white handkerchief with which he wiped his sweaty face. This trial clearly did not appear to be going his way.

A large roar of approval then came from the crowd as Congolese independence leader, Patrice Lumumba, rose slowly from his seat and walked purposefully to the podium. Dressed in a black Mao-style suit; his thick, round-rimmed glasses glistened in the sun. Also noticeable was his uneven hair with the trademark parting on the left side.

Lumumba quietened the crowd, and then launched into an angry tirade in which his Lingala and French intonation came out strongly, waving his hands energetically throughout his verdict.

"Fellow After Africans! I am here as a judge on the Council of the Wise representing Central Africa. I want to note that I myself was a victim of the very system that Cecil Rhodes embodied: imperialism. You all know the story of my martyrdom, when the Belgians and Americans colluded with the treacherous Moise Tshombe – happily now in the Hades of African autocrats in After Africa –

to assassinate me, and hand the leadership of my country to the Western-backed dictator Mobutu Sese Seko, who then unleashed a ruinous 31-year reign of terror on my beloved Congolese people. Mobutu is also now thankfully in the Hades of Autocrats. Rhodes was a contemporary of Belgian King Léopold who turned my country into his private fiefdom. He claimed to own the Congo, fellow After Africans, killing ten million Congolese – an estimated half of the population at the time – in the process, through slave labour and torture. This included cutting off the hands and genitals of labourers and flogging them to death for not producing sufficient rubber on his slave plantations. It is this very system that is now on trial in After Africa."

As the Congolese liberation hero used a grey handkerchief to wipe sweat from his face, the crowd thundered their approval.

Lumumba gazed directly at the shaken Cecil Rhodes. "This man had described Africa north of the Limpopo as South Africa's 'natural hinterland,' as if it was terra incognito even to the people who had lived there for centuries! He wanted to build a railway from the Cape to Cairo in order to paint the whole map of Africa red, in those days the colour of the imperial power. We are so happy that the sun did finally set on the British empire, and that

England became the legatee of a declining estate, suffering one of the most spectacular declines of any great power in history. Rhodes's heirs included the country's white leaders, as well as the South African Federated Chamber of Industries and the South African Foreign Trade Organisation, who sought to exploit mining and other opportunities north of the Limpopo. Even in the post-apartheid era, we hear that South African business interests still often talk as if they are determined to follow in Rhodes's colossal footsteps. Mostly white South African businesses have fanned out across the continent in areas like mining, banking, retail, communications, armaments, and insurance, making references to a 'sense of pioneering' and describing themselves as 'an army on the move'. This is the legacy that Cecil Rhodes and his ilk have bequeathed: he effectively opened up Southern Africa to Western exploitation."

Lumumba poured some water into a glass from a large wooden jug and drank it.

"I just want to say a brief word about one of the Counsel for Damnation, in order to inject a certain nuance into our debate. Though Olive Schreiner condemned Rhodes yesterday, and advocated the rights of black people, she had befriended him before falling out with the arch-imperialist, and often referred to black people in her novels in offensive terms like 'kaffirs.' Even in her day, the term 'natives' was in more common usage. South Africa's African National Congress – then called the South African Native National Congress – had, after all, appeared on the scene eight years before Schreiner's death in 1920, and there were black political leaders emerging in her own era. I must also question Schreiner's naïve early belief that British imperialism could ever have been a force for good, since the very basis of imperialism is to subjugate the rights of black people and 'savages' considered inferior to whites. Schreiner's approach is thus that of a paternalistic white liberal, viewing Africans as victims unable to exercise their full agency, while white imperialists remain the sole source of their salvation. I think our history of struggle to liberate Africa from colonial rule disproves Schreiner's approach."

Loud applause rang out around the stadium again, as Olive Schreiner's face turned bright red, even as Stanlake Samkange tried to console her.

Lumumba continued his fiery verdict, "Having criticised the Counsel for Damnation, I think it is only fair also to criticise one of the Counsel for Salvation. Nelson Mandela – a deserving hero of our liberation struggle in the Herebefore, who has been much deservedly venerated here in After Africa – indelibly and unwisely linked his name to that of Cecil Rhodes in the Mandela Rhodes Foundation in 2003. It is shocking that in Rhodes House in

Oxford, Mandela's picture has a white bust of Cecil Rhodes lurking behind him, as well as a painting of each hanging side by side. Surely, Jews would not have established a Herzl Hitler foundation, so what is this monstrosity of Mandela Rhodes?"

The crowd again burst into uncontrolled laughter and spontaneous applause, before Judge Elias restored calm. Mandela shook his head bitterly.

"Mandela, in his address yesterday, drew shocking similarities between himself and Cecil Rhodes. The contrasts between Rhodes and Mandela, however, are enormous. While Rhodes was one of the greatest imperialists of the nineteenth century, Mandela was one of the greatest liberators of the twentieth. While Mandela struggled financially as a lawyer and spent 27 years of his life in jail protesting the evil injustices of the apartheid regime, Rhodes lived a wealthy life aggressively promoting the interests of the British Empire through harsh and unjust means for which he was never held accountable until now. While Rhodes visited unimaginable cruelty upon black populations in South Africa, Zambia, and Zimbabwe, Mandela was the very embodiment of national reconciliation. While Rhodes is now widely despised across Africa as an aggressive racist, Mandela remains one of the greatest moral figures in death and in the Herebefore. While Rhodes died a relatively early death at the age of 48 and effectively drank himself to death, the teetotal Mandela lived a long life until his arrival here. I think it is vital to set the historical record straight."

As the crowd roared their approval, Mandela fidgeted stiffly in his chair.

"Mandela effectively rehabilitated a grotesque imperialist of the nineteenth century. Surely, Madiba, you could have used the Rhodes Trust and its £10 million blood money to pursue good deeds without forever linking your name to that of Cecil Rhodes? The Rhodes Trust surely needed your name more than you needed their money! Mr Mandela has surely taken the African concept of ubuntu too far in rehabilitating an evil figure that Africans really should have condemned to the pit latrine of history. I hope we can do this today in After Africa."

More applause followed and Elias quietened the crowd, before gently urging Lumumba to conclude his remarks, noting, "Patrice, please remember that it is Cecil Rhodes, not Nelson Mandela, who is on trial."

Lumumba nodded, then ended his verdict, "Thank the gods of After Africa that Cecil Rhodes never found the diamonds that currently exist in contemporary Zimbabwe, otherwise cynical Western governments, led by formerly Great Britain, would have insisted on a white minority government continuing to rule over blacks in perpetuity in

Southern Rhodesia. I conclude by upholding the charges of mass murder, racism, and theft of land against Cecil Rhodes, and will leave my other three remaining members of the Council of the Wise to deal with some of the other charges."

As Lumumba soaked up the applause of the audience and took his seat on the giant golden throne, the elegant Ruth First rose slowly from her chair to make her way to the podium, amidst deafening shouts of "Sis Ruth! Sis Ruth!" She then launched into her verdict.

"Good afternoon, After Africans. I am keenly aware of the responsibility that Africa's gods have placed on our shoulders today, and I am proud to represent Southern Africa on the Council of the Wise. This is significantly the African sub-region that was most affected by Rhodes's imperial greed. As many of you already know, I was martyred to the cause of Pan-Africanism in the Herebefore when an apartheid letter bomb killed me in Maputo. I thus arrived earlier than expected in After Africa. As I have often said, I count myself an African, and there is no cause I hold more dear.

"Cecil Rhodes perfected the exploitative migrant labour system in Southern Africa to feed his avarice through his gold and diamond mines. I consistently believed that one had to end the system of economic exploitation in South Africa by cutting off its regional and external sinews. I thus focused my research on labour recruitment policies in Namibia – effectively a colony of South Africa for eight decades – which saw blacks holed up in Bantustans and forced to provide labour for mines, farms, and factories. This was a system pioneered by Mr Rhodes. I also studied the role of Mozambican miners, which strengthened my belief that cutting off the guaranteed supply of migrant labour to South Africa from neighbouring countries would do great damage to the South African economy. However, having realised the destruction this would also wreak on labour-exporting Southern African countries, I proposed that this disengagement be done gradually.

"As a journalist for 15 years, I wrote exposés of exploited black miners and farm-workers, and argued strongly that the structure of capitalist exploitation in South Africa ultimately shaped the context in which all these struggles took place. This structure too was something that Rhodes helped pioneer. I was also an early supporter of economic sanctions against the apartheid regime, as I realised that its dependence on foreign capital was its Achilles heel. The expansion of the Oppenheimer group – headed by Counsel for Salvation, Harry Oppenheimer, here with us on stage – to Southern Africa and beyond, further resulted in South Africa's growing interdependence with the sub-regional economy and their dependence on us.

"Counsel for Damnation, Stanlake Samkange, has already described well Cecil Rhodes's exploitation of underpaid slave workers, packing over 11 000 black miners like sardines into inhumane, dog-patrolled, barracks surrounded with barbed wire; and his support of draconian labour laws like the 'strop bill' that allowed the flogging of workers. Rhodes is thus undoubtedly guilty of the crime of exploiting and enslaving black workers, and I believe that he should be convicted as a racist mass murderer who stole land from black people across Southern Africa. I thank you for listening."

As First walked back to her seat to loud applause, she once more pumped her fist in the air and shouted, "Amandla! Amandla!" and drew even wilder cheers from the crowd.

First took her seat on her giant throne. Maya Angelou then rose gracefully to take her place at the podium. She wore an elegant orange, green, and black *Kente* dress with matching headgear, in honour of her sojourn in Kwame Nkrumah's Ghana in the Herebefore. She launched into her verdict in her melodious, firm African-American voice, "I am honoured to represent the North American Diaspora here as part of After Africa's Council of the Wise. Since this is a trial of imperialism and its greatest proponent, I would like to read a poem in honour of those who resisted imperialism and its evil twin – slavery – which took my ancestors and at least 12 million other Africans to the Western hemisphere. I will leave our last judge, Toussaint L'Ouverture, to fill in details of this sordid trade. My poem is titled 'Still I Rise,' and tells of the tragedies and triumphs of the black struggle over five centuries:

You may write me down in history
With your bitter, twisted lies,
You may trod me in the very dirt
But still, like dust, I'll rise.

The audience roared its approval.

"Let me start my verdict by saying that the lynching of black men by Rhodes's brutal soldiers in Matabeleland and Mashonaland is something that I find especially odious, given the similar history of castration and lynching of black men in the US: about 4 000 African-Americans were lynched in the South between 1877 and 1950. My country is one that Rhodes greatly admired and to which he left the bulk of his scholarships at Oxford University in his will. This was, of course, a vainglorious attempt to create a 'Heaven's breed' of lily-white 'Masters of the Universe.' As a former professor, I would thus like to limit my remarks to the legacy of Rhodes's scholarship scheme, as well as recall a private visit I undertook to his birthplace, Bishop's Strotford in England. I will therefore focus largely on the charge of egotism and a vainglorious quest for immortality. Rhodes had, after all, expected to be remembered in the Herebefore for four thousand years. "He had said, notoriously, that 'I find I am human, but would like to live after my death.' Rhodes named two countries after himself in a vainglorious quest for immortality. His legacy can be seen in the Herebefore especially in the cities of Cape Town, Kimberly, Grahamstown, Oxford, and Bishop's Stortford. There is a large Rhodes memorial, and a statue that was toppled at the University of Cape Town (UCT), as well as another that was 'beheaded' by protesters near the UCT campus; an equestrian statue in Kimberley; Rhodes University in Grahamstown; the grandiose Rhodes House in Oxford; a statue towering over two British Kings – George V and Edward VII – on the High Street in Oxford, which Oriel college announced that it would take down; and a museum at his birthplace in Bishop's Stortford. Rhodes's obsessive quest for immortality saw him encourage his associates and supporters to deify his name and image.

"These were all efforts to worship Rhodes as a colossus, whether looking down broodingly on shoppers on Oxford's busy High Street, or on the inhabitants of the southernmost tip of Africa in Cape Town, or on conquered people in Zimbabwe's Matopos Hills, where he lies buried. He dreamed of building a railway from the Cape to Cairo, and sought to bring as much of Africa as possible under the imperial Union Jack of his native Britain. Rhodes's country honoured him and repaid his imperial service: during the centenary of his birth in 1953, Britain's Queen Mother and Princess Margaret visited the then Southern Rhodesia, and the Royal Mint produced 125 000 silver crown pieces with Rhodes's head. A memorial tablet for Rhodes was also unveiled at Westminster Abbey. The Rhodes Chair of Race Relations, established at Oxford University in 1953, is perhaps one of the greatest oxymorons that one can imagine, as Rhodes destroyed rather than promoted race relations."

The crowd burst into derisive laughter. Angelou drank from a gourd of palm wine, before continuing.

"As earlier noted, what is important to remember about the Rhodes scholarships, set up in 1903, is that black and other Southern Africans have benefitted less from it than white Americans, white Australians, and white Canadians. And as you know, this sub-region is where Rhodes built up the wealth that funded the scholarship named after him. And in Southern Africa, it was white South Africans who benefitted from the scholarships, disproportionately.

The South African scholarships have thus effectively served as a form of white affirmative action for over a century. Students from schools listed in Rhodes's will – none of which admitted either blacks or girls until the 1980s – continued to obtain four of the nine South African scholarships. And bear in mind that the Rhodes trustees themselves were not always progressive, and were mostly pale white males.

"As apartheid South Africa became increasingly diplomatically isolated, American Rhodes scholars led petitions and protests to increase black representation on the scheme, and even to cut off scholarships to the country altogether. This pressure eventually led the Rhodes trustees in Oxford to go to court belatedly to force the four whites-only schools for boys to admit blacks and girls. It was only in 1976 that the first black Rhodes scholar and the first female Rhodes scholar were chosen, 72 years after the first lily-white South African scholars went up to Oxford. Only four black scholars were thus selected in the first 80 years of a scheme that still appears to be more albinocratic than meritocratic. Rhodes himself was not reputed to have been a particularly good student. It took him eight years at Oxford to achieve what was politely called a 'gentleman's pass.' It was often said that Rhodes could not have become a Rhodes scholar!"

Angelou drank some more palm wine from the

brown gourd as she soaked up the applause and laughter from the animated crowd.

Now really enjoying herself, she continued, "My final observations concern a private visit I undertook to the Bishop's Stortford Museum. This tour provided me with further evidence of how Rhodes's exploits have been largely forgotten, even in his own home town. I visited this small, sleepy English town in Hertfordshire with charming pubs and St. Michael's Church, where Rhodes's father had been the vicar. In the museum, indigenous African music played in the background amidst African axes, shields, and other weapons forged by African blacksmiths. African drums and baskets were also on display. There were depictions of slavery and imperialism, and at least some recognition that Rhodes's legacy had been contested, even during his own lifetime.

"Numerous pictures of Rhodes littered the room: him growing up as a child; as prime minister of the Cape Colony; and with Lord Kitchener during the Anglo-Boer war. I was told by the guide that even though many schoolchildren visited the museum, many English pupils do not learn about Rhodes, he is not in their curriculum. Of far greater interest in the same building was the Rhodes Art complex, which offered theatre, comedies, and music at sessions on Fridays that they spectacularly miscalled 'Rhodes

Rocks.' It is this entertainment that sustained the very quiet museum, and many in the town clearly thought about Rhodes more in terms of entertainment than in the context of imperialism. The commercialisation and packaging of this ruthless businessman in his English hometown was perhaps the ultimate irony in the vainglorious quest for immortality of a megalomaniac plunderer-politician. We hear from beyond the grave that there are efforts totally to eliminate Rhodes's name from this museum complex. Mr Rhodes is clearly guilty as charged for the crime of egotism and a vainglorious quest for immortality. I rest my case."

Amidst wild applause, Cecil sat frozen in the middle of the stage, clearly shattered by the desolation of his legacy in his English hometown. Angelou walked slowly and proudly to her seat.

The large crowd waited with bated breath, realising that only one vote was needed for a unanimous verdict, and silence descended on the stadium as a golden sun began to set in the background of this momentous trial. Cecil sat motionless in the centre of the stage, fearing the worst, and clearly physically and emotionally drained from the deliberations.

General Toussaint L'Ouverture – dressed in the military uniform of revolutionary Haitian Black Jacobins, namely a richly embroidered military jacket with a white sash across it and golden lapels on the shoulders, and a sword by his side – then rose dramatically and marched to the podium, generating wild applause. Then the general immediately launched into his speech.

"I am honoured to be here to represent the Caribbean and South American diasporas in this important trial in After Africa. Since I was the leader of the only successful slave rebellion in history before the grave, and one that created the world's first black republic, only the second independent republic in the Caribbean and the Americas at the time, I think it is appropriate to make a link between slavery and the system of imperialism for which Cecil Rhodes stands accused. Slavery was undoubtedly Europe's original sin against Africa. European locusts – explorers, slavers, planters, merchants, missionaries, imperialists – arrived in Africa in the fifteenth century, and for the next five centuries, ravaged the continent. The agricultural sector, from which most Africans sustained their livelihoods, was destroyed, famines proliferated, and the greatest migration in human history was enforced.

"Since imperialism as a system is also on trial as well as its most symbolic representative, it is worth noting that colonialism was the continuation of slavery by other means. Enslavement dehumanised Africans globally, and provided the racist justifications and economic methods that were used to implement colonialism on the grounds that Africans could not yet stand on their own feet in the difficult conditions of Western 'civilization.' Three and a half centuries of European enslavement of Africans to work on plantations in the Caribbean and the Americas thus flowed seamlessly into a century of European imperialism on the African continent. Both systems involved profit-driven exploitation – cloaked under perverse justifications of a *mission civilisatrice* – which blamed African victims for their own misfortunes, while the whole project was legitimised by Western leaders, capitalists, churches, and scientists from slave-trading Britain, the US, France, Spain, Portugal, the Netherlands, Sweden, and Denmark."

The crowd erupted into thunderous applause, as l'Ouverture waited patiently for the clapping to die down before concluding.

"Millions of the most productive African men and women – typically between the ages of 15 and 35 – were thus enslaved in their prime, and an entire continent was depopulated of some of its most productive workforce. African agriculture suffered greatly, and famines increased in some areas, as slave-hunters and warriors were prioritised over farmers and entrepreneurs. Slavery effectively arrested human and socioeconomic development, and intra-regional trade across Africa. Imperialism continued the damage, and crippled and deformed African, Caribbean, and South American countries at birth. Both systems, however, provided the capital for Europe and America's industrial revolutions. The industrialisation of the West was thus literally built on the backs of slavery and colonialism. It is therefore clear that Rhodes is guilty of racism, mass murder, and grand theft of Africa's wealth and land. He must face the stiffest penalty in After Africa for defiling the land of our ancestors and its peoples."

As dusk fell, pandemonium broke out. Cecil Rhodes dramatically fainted in the middle of the stage, having realised that the verdict was unanimous. Cold water was poured on his face, and the arch-imperialist was helped back to his feet to stand to attention to await his sentence. Judge Elias then asked the six other Council members to rise together and remain standing while he read out his verdict. The jubilant crowd continued their raucous noise, as Elias quietened the now thunderous stadium after what seemed like an eternity. He then opened his large well worn Book of Judgment and started to read slowly as total silence descended on the fifth heaven of After Africa.

"Cecil Rhodes, you have witnessed the judgment that has been delivered by our six eminent judges representing all parts of Africa and its diaspora. We have conducted a fair trial according to the laws of the gods of After Africa, and you have been given a chance to respond to the charges and to be defended by two Counsel for Salvation against the charges of our two Counsel for Damnation.

"You have been found guilty of all five charges: mass murder; racism; grand theft of Africa's natural resources and land; exploitation and enslavement of African workers; and egotism and a vainglorious quest for immortality. You are thus herby unanimously convicted beyond any reasonable doubt. My three-part final judgment is as much a verdict on yourself as on the system of imperialism that you embody. First, your remains in the Herebefore are to be disinterred from the Matopos Hills in Zimbabwe where they currently lie buried, and transported back by angels in the sixth heaven to your birthplace of Bishop's Stortford for reburial. Your physical remains continue to defile the soil of Africa, and the spirit of our ancestors must now be allowed to rest. Second, the gods will arrange that your assets be confiscated in the Herebefore and used as reparations to compensate the descendants of the victims of your crimes in Southern Africa, specifically in South Africa, Zimbabwe, and Zambia. Finally, you will be arrested immediately and sent down to the Hades of African Autocrats from which you ascended after 120 years in Limbo. You shall remain in eternal damnation facing hellfire as just punishment for your crimes. Thank you all for your cooperation, and may the deities in the seventh heaven bless Africa and its diaspora."

The crowd in After Africa burst into spontaneous jubilation and some stormed the stage. The seven judges exited the stadium in a ritual procession followed by the four Counsel for Damnation and Salvation. As total darkness descended on the Fifth Heaven, everyone agreed that they had just witnessed the trial for all ages in After Africa. A sober and trembling Cecil John Rhodes was put in chains and handcuffs, and led away to his fate.

A note on sources

This historical novella has necessarily relied on my own published work and edited books, as well as various sources which I would like to acknowledge: On Cecil Rhodes and the Rhodes Trust, the following books were particularly helpful: Anthony Kenny (ed.) *The History of the Rhodes Trust* (Oxford: Oxford University Press, 2001); Bernard Magubane, *The Making of a Racist State* (Asmara: Africa World Press, 1996); Paul Maylam, *The Cult of Rhodes: Remembering an Imperialist in Africa* (Cape Town: David Philip, 2005); Kalim Rajab (ed.), *A Man of Africa: The Political Thought of Harry Oppenheimer* (Cape Town: Penguin Random House, 2017); Robert Rotberg, *The Founder: Cecil Rhodes and the Pursuit of Power* (Johannesburg: Jonathan Ball, 2002); Antony Thomas, *Rhodes: The Race for Africa* (Johannesburg: Jonathan Ball, 1996); and

Philip Ziegler, *Legacy: Cecil Rhodes, The Rhodes Trust and Rhodes Scholarships* (New Haven and London: Yale University Press, 2008). Other useful sources were: James Currey, *Africa Writes Back: The African Writers Series and The Launch of African Literature* (Oxford: James Currey, 2008); Anne V. Adams and Esi Sutherland-Addy (eds.), *The Legacy of Efua Sutherland: Pan-African Cultural Activism* (Accra and Oxford: Ayebia Clarke Publishing Limited, 2007); and Simon Broughton, Mark Ellingham, and Jon Lusk, *The Rough Guide to World Music: Africa & Middle East* (London: Rough Guides Ltd, 2006), third edition. *The Economist*, "Hell: A Very Rough Guide," 22 December 2012; and standard academic and Wikipedia summarized histories of Africa were also helpful.